*"Carmen Harra is a talented, deeply
for life coupled with her vast metaph*

— **Arielle Ford**, au

MW01595290

*In this delightfully written book, Dr. Carmen brings us sensible, easy ways to
increased mind-body-spirit health. From her "Seven Guiding Principles" of
Awareness, Proactivity, Balance, Joy, Togetherness, Nature, and Creating Good
Choices/Karma, she weaves a joyful and focused plan to holistic health and
awareness in daily living. As a curriculum writer and CEO of an education
non-profit co-founded by Neale Donald Walsch, I am always looking for inspired,
practical application methods to bring peace, harmony and love of self to whole
new levels. This book gifts that to Dr. Carmen's readers. Bravo to us all – see
how this book can shift your body-mind-spirit into "…the grandest version of the
greatest vision of yourself…" now! (quote from Conversations with God books by
N.D.Walsch)*

— **Linda Lee Ratto**, Ed.M., SNS CEO, www.SchooloftheNewSpirituality.com

*"This book explores a plethora of insights, including Mindful Awareness, to
help one plan and create a balanced, happy, healthy life using body-mind-
spirit methods."*

— **Linda Mackenzie**, author of *Help Yourself Heal with Self-Hypnosis*
and Founder of HealthyLife.Net - All Positive Talk Radio

*"Dr. Carmen Harra is one of the most superbly gifted counselors on the
planet. Her prognostication skills and accuracy are second to none. All
of Dr. Harra's books are packed with deep insights and profound truths.
The Trinity of Health is no exception. Read this book, and it will change
your life."*

— **Jon Sweeney**, Founder of Coherence Therapy

*"Dr Carmen Harra, Ph.D., has created an important template in her latest book
for your continued growth and evolution. With important ideas and information
on all aspects of your life, from reconnecting to Mother Earth to a food plan for
grounding you in a healthy way. Most important, bringing more Balance to you in
mind, body and Spirit!"*

— **Scott Cluthe**, *Positively Incorrect!*, Lime Radio on Sirius Satellite Radio

*"Carmen Harra has heart, knowledge and desire, three vital things needed and
discussed in her latest book The Trinity of Health. Carmen's writing keeps it
simple for anyone to find their health and spirit and keep it authentic. Carmen
is by far a teacher that KNOWS how to incorporate heart knowledge and desire
and assist our planet the people that live here a better way to live and make
healthier choices."*

— **Cameron Steele**, Contact Talk Radio Network www.contacttalkradio.com

ISBN: 1-4196-6562-6
ISBN-13: 978-1419665622

Visit www.booksurge.com to order additional copies.

The
TRINITY
Of
HEALTH

Align body, mind and soul
in order to achieve health and happiness
for Your Whole Life

By
Carmen Harra, Ph.D.

With
Allie Swain and
Mona F. Muresan, Ph.D

TABLE OF CONTENTS

PART ONE:

SEVEN GUIDING PRINCIPLES

PART TWO:

HOW TO EAT HEALTHILY — AND JOYFULLY!!

This book is dedicated to the memory of our parents, Alexandrina and Victor Muresan, for their divine inspiration and for implementing in us the virtue of togetherness and family unity.

"When Health is absent...
Wisdom cannot reveal itself,
art cannot become manifested;
strength cannot be exerted,
wealth is useless and
reason is powerless."

— *Herophiles, 300 BC*

FOREWORD

By: Dr. Adrian Sangeorzan, M.D.

One of the fundamental dangers in the world today seems to be losing our balance. We lose our balance all the time: when we eat and when we drink, when we work and when we think. And very often we lose our balance when our emotions get the better of us, and we lose our tempers or become depressed. Many people think less and less for themselves, and more and more often they think other people's thoughts instead. These thoughts infiltrate our own thinking and judgment daily through advertisements, films, newspapers, television, etc. As a result, our confusion only becomes greater.

We eat compulsively, and too much, as if this is the only thing left to do. We feel all sorts of diffuse symptoms because our own thoughts and emotions often are in contradiction with each other. We have created a world where we easily swallow pills for just about anything. We take in food and ideas that have been too processed. We are constantly waiting for miracles

— miracles that elude us because we are clueless as to how we, ourselves, might make them happen.

The new generation seems to be more and more interested in a virtual world where virtual problems and solutions do not always correspond to the real world. In this context, it is easier to see the dark and inevitable path of alienation opening before us. We run the risk of becoming alienated from our true selves and from everything good around us, unless we decide to defend ourselves.

If you enter a bookstore, it is difficult to find a book about us the way we are. It is especially difficult to find a book that offers real and intelligent solutions. There is a jungle of material out there, and more often than not, what we choose to read will only add to the confusion.

Dr. Carmen Harra's new book is a must. It is a comprehensive book, necessary to everyone more than ever. Dr. Harra has her feet firmly planted in the ground, and her head up in a sacred place from where our spirit and emotions can receive the best and healthiest nourishment.

Being a complex personality with deep roots in the culture and traditions of Europe, Dr. Harra knew where to look, how to find, and how to keep the best and healthiest of everything she has ever accumulated while reading, living, traveling, as well as from practicing on the most diverse clients.

Her book is well structured and provides answers to many questions that keep torturing us on a conscious or subconscious level. And even more importantly, it offers practical solutions to our most pressing problems. These problems challenge us today, both on an individual level and collectively, since our society in its turn suffers a parallel alienation from most of the things that are good and healthy.

We know that we are becoming more and more overweight, sedentary, and depressed. We are becoming less communicative, and less open to others and to the good around us. We know that we need to eat less, choose healthier foods and exercise more. We know that we need to have healthier thoughts and emotions. We know that we need to be more loving, and to communicate more with the people around us.

We know all this, and yet we do not do it because it is all so overwhelming, and we do not know where to start or how to proceed. There is hardly anybody out there to teach us in a practical, easy, no-nonsense way. When you read Carmen Harra's *The Trinity of Health*, you will find a real teacher. You will have the awakening of true direction being revealed to you.

Carmen Harra knew how to choose from the varied multitude of spiritual and medical theories and concepts. She chose the things that can help us the most, and that we can all adopt on a daily basis. She chose the things that will help us navigate our recurring ocean of daily temptations and traps and finally emerge whole, healthy and happy.

Dr. Adrian Sangeorzan, M.D.,
author of *Over the Lifeline*

INTRODUCTION

by Carmen Harra, Ph.D.

Based on scientific analysis, we know that the human molecule can survive up to a thousand years. Yet why does the human body degenerate and deteriorate so quickly? How is it that the trees live for hundreds of years?

Being human, we primarily blame gravity for our aging process, and we blame our death on the fact that, as our energy changes, our physical bodies transform and decay. But why do some of us live to be 100 years old, to be creative, and live a dynamic life well into our 90's, while others begin to deteriorate in our 50's and 60's, and are ready to let go of life?

In order to answer such questions, we must begin to look within and reflect upon our quality of life. We must begin to acknowledge all the things we do to ourselves — from the way that we think, to the way we care for ourselves, and most importantly, to our eating habits.

Life is a process: living longer, living healthier, living more spiritually, and living a better life are all processes.

This book is about examining the guiding principles and laws that lead to a better, longer life, and then applying them in a very practical way in order to achieve that. We are at a time of evolution when all of us are trying to increase our lifespan. We're all trying to create the fullest, healthiest, richest and happiest life. Finding the keys to that happier, healthier life is the purpose of this book.

In order to project what changes we want to make in our future, we must first begin with taking a look into the past. In my experience, as I mentioned in my earlier books, *Everyday Karma* and *Decoding Destiny*, the most reliable prophet for your future is your past. So that we can predict how to create a better future for all of us, in terms of living a whole and healthy life, we have to first look back to the way we lived in ancient times.

Thousands of years ago we didn't have prescription medications. We didn't even have doctors, as we know them today. Thousands of years ago we used to live as nomads. The way we survived was by eating straight from the Earth, meditating and praying, and being more connected to God.

We used to live very long lives. If you read the Bible, it talks about Abraham who had a child when he was 800 years old. This is something that we cannot even comprehend at this level of our evolution. It's almost as if we lost track of the fact that it was possible. This is one of the things that the Bible shows us: that it was possible to live a thousand years in another time, thousands and thousands of years ago. So why isn't it possible in the technological world of today?

We live in a world where everything happens quickly; a world of fast food that is filled with emotional excess. It's also a world of Prozac and all kinds of pills, where we're more neurotic and crazy than ever before. We are full of anxiety and stress. We're so stressed that we can't seem to stop long enough to take care of ourselves. In many ways, we are disconnected from ourselves, from our bodies. That means we're also disconnected from the beauty within — and from the God within us.

This book is here to help you reconnect to you, to improve the relationship you have with food, and the relationship you have with the Spirit. Food is Spirit, because everything exists in a totality: what you eat, what you think, what you project in the universe, how you meditate, how you return to nature, is all connected. Everything is part of a whole.

All the advice in books today about living healthily begin with the idea of taking time for yourself, which includes taking time for nature, and time for meditation. Books on spirituality often help you eliminate disturbances in the brain by helping you to reconnect with your thought process — how you think — so you can change what you think. This applies to everything you do in life. If your life is not going well, it's usually because of stagnation and emotional problems. Some of these problems actually come from the way people eat, and from the way they relate to themselves and the world around them.

This is a book about togetherness, living a longer life, and being happier in the process. By knowing how to treat yourself, and how to relate to the world around you, that alone can establish the basis for happiness. If you look at the ancient teachings of Ayurveda, the science of life, it shows how you can live a long life by learning how to relate to nature. Ayurveda says the same thing as the Bible about our ability to live much longer lives. Ayurvedic teachings show you how to handle emotions, how to avoid unhealthy foods, how to use sound therapy, how to use nature for the healing of your spirit. More importantly, it shows you how to slow down and keep a stressful life from taking control of your thinking. We know now, from many sources, that stress is definitely one of the killers of our mind, body and spirit.

So in summary, this book is a guide on how to create happiness and wholesome habits for living, based on universal principles and the tools of life, the main tools of human survival. <u>This is not a book about dieting.</u> If you look at the word "diet," the first three letters of the word spell out the word "die"! You don't want to die(t) — you want to live!

Therefore, this book refers to food as a vital part of healthy living. It refers to eating for health and joy. Losing excess weight will be a bonus that will follow if you start putting into practice our guiding principles and practical recommendations.

Food is definitely a fabulous way to heal, and this book shows how that's possible, by connecting the eating process to the mental process. The principles of this book refer to and draw upon all the basic spiritual laws of the Universe, such as awareness, being proactive, and visualizing a picture of your life in order to create a life that is whole. This book is about "holiness," about totality, about the wholeness we can find in enjoying and celebrating life. There's no better celebration than when we call together in harmony the three parts of us: body, mind and soul — the trinity of health.

"We're not human beings having a
spiritual experience,
We're spiritual beings having a
human experience."
(Source Unknown)

INTRODUCTION

by Allie Swain and Mona F. Muresan

We are more than just our biology. We are not simply a collection of biochemical reactions. We need to connect with the totality of who we are. Many books focus on the body: what to eat, how to exercise. And yet for most of us, it is so hard to change our daily routine, to trade in what we know for what we don't know.

We read so many books that contain profound wisdom about how to live a better, healthier life, but invariably we are left with the same frustrating question every time: "This is all great, but what do I actually do with this information? How can I understand it, implement it, and integrate it into my daily life? Please give me some concrete, simple steps — something I can do every day!" This book was designed to answer those questions in a pragmatic and practical way, giving you both general guidelines as well as specific steps you can go out and put into practice today!

*"You must understand the whole of life,
not just one little part of it."*
— J. Krishnamurti

This book is about your **_whole_** life in several different ways:

— It gives you a plan you can use for your entire life. It's not about changing your diet for two weeks, or starting an exercise plan for three months. It's about integrating healthy habits into every day and every year of your life.

— It offers you ways of integrating all the different aspects of your life into one "whole" that works, which is the sum of all the parts. It's about integrating healthy eating, exercise, weight loss, relationships, work and free time into your life. It illustrates how you can attain health and wholeness, not by being obsessed about one part of your life, but by keeping a healthy balance, and seeing how everything fits into a bigger picture.

— It's about the importance of eating more "whole" foods; real foods that are closer to nature, less refined, less processed, more alive.

This book will talk about spirituality in a non-denominational way because we are body, mind and soul. We will mention and connect to ideas and traditions that stem from many different sources, including Christianity, Buddhism, and the Kaballah. Even if you consider yourself a totally "non-religious" person, we believe you will still find these ideas and practical suggestions helpful. These are universal guiding principles for a healthy life, regardless of your religious affiliation. When in doubt, simply try them and you will find that put into practice, they do work.

It's truly amazing that in the Western world we, who can afford to eat better, actually choose to eat "junk" food. One of the aims of this book is to help you find easy options — to make it easier to choose differently, and to eat more healthily.

In *Part One*, we begin by introducing Seven Guiding Principles for wholeness, one for each chapter. We call them interchangeably "principles" or "laws." At the end of each chapter will be a section that will offer specific suggestions on how to actually integrate the guiding principle into your daily life.

Part Two is where you will find more practical tips on how to incorporate healthy habits into your daily routine, including choosing more nutritious alternatives for every meal. This will make your transition to a healthier lifestyle a real pleasure.

At the end of the book, we will have a section entitled *Where Do You Go From Here?* that will offer suggestions and examples on how to use this book, such as, "A Principle A Day." For instance, you would start with the Seven Guiding Principles, and make a plan to focus on one principle each day of the week. We will also include a Seven-Day Program to provide you with the structure you need to get started.

In Western societies today, we have pretty much eliminated many of the big killer diseases of the past, such as tuberculosis, cholera, and smallpox. And yet, ironically, rather than having less need for doctors, medicine and hospitals, we are spending more money on medical care than ever. Far from being the healthiest on Earth, people living in the so-called "developed world" have many serious health problems, many of which are caused in part by lifestyle factors: poor diets (based largely on "fake" food), lack of exercise and stress. This book is about reclaiming the trinity of our health, and integrating healthy habits into our lives each day, every day, for our whole life.

This book is about taking responsibility for your health and well-being. Therefore, **CONSULT YOUR DOCTOR OR HEALTH CARE PRACTITIONER BEFORE CHANGING YOUR DIET AND EXERCISE REGIMEN!**

The information given here is intended as a reference volume only, not as a medical manual.

The information given here is designed to help you make informed choices about your health, diet, fitness and exercise program. It is not intended as a substitute for professional fitness and medical advice. If you suspect you have a medical problem, we urge you to seek competent medical help. As with all exercise programs and changes in diet, you should seek your doctor's approval before you begin.

Some of the central ideas and concepts of this book will be presented several times from different angles. This process of repetition is by design; it will help you recognize new information and integrate it better and faster into your own thinking.

PART ONE:

SEVEN GUIDING PRINCIPLES

Chapter One

Guiding Principle #1: Cultivate Awareness
Know What You Do and Do What You Know

Awareness is the first law of life. In order to achieve something positive, you need the principle of Awareness. The majority of us have no awareness in our actions or intentions on a daily basis. We just go with whatever's happening, and as a result, we get too trapped in our daily routines and in our emotions. We stop at the corner market and buy whatever kind of food is available. We ignore our body's need for exercise and give no thought to the way we eat. We eat walking down the street, standing over the counter or the computer keyboard, in our cars or on the train. We ignore our well-being totally because we think that there's no time for it, or we assume it's something that will come "naturally," without any effort on our part.

Everything in life comes through awareness. That's why awareness is the first and most significant law of all, because if you're aware of what you've done to harm yourself, you can make a plan to heal. You can become creative about your life, so you can be clear about your intentions. You can build your life. The more aware you become, the more you realize the mistakes of your past, and the more clearly you see what you must change. You can establish new patterns, and break through negative habits. Some of the most significant moments in life are when we are able to see and break through a negative pattern, and change the course of our lives.

Awareness comes when we contemplate ourselves more deeply. It requires a lot of introspection, and even study, about the quality of life and what that means. When we look back and see how much we as human beings have changed from the way we behaved towards ourselves in the ancient past, it's almost incredible. We live in a society, in a world that is moving very fast. Everything happens very quickly. When you do things quickly, you don't have time to become aware. Awareness is always linked to stillness — to the concept of meditating and taking time out, of stopping to listen to the signals from yourself, from your body. If you don't ever meditate or take time out to tune in to yourself, you're not living with awareness.

Awareness is realizing when something has to be changed. Awareness goes hand-in-hand with the idea of growth and making positive changes. We all have to make changes in our lives, and if we don't pay attention to the signals from our body, the body will continue to let us know somehow that something is wrong. The way that the body will tell us something is wrong by experiencing pain or a chronic symptom or by having a nightmare.

When you wake up in the middle of the night because you've had a nightmare and you don't know the source of the nightmare, the subconscious is telling you that something is not right, and that it's time you look inward. Going within, you have to be sincere and take an honest look at your habits, your way of living. There are beautiful ways of living that have withstood for thousands of years. The purpose of this book is to go back to the beginning, to the origin of the beautiful laws of living, the laws of a healthy, happy life.

Awareness comes first. You're first aware when you wake up in the morning. With awareness you can establish a new ritual in your life, for example, by taking a walk in the morning, taking a couple of deep breaths, learning how to meditate and calm yourself down. Never allow your daily routine to overwhelm you, or pressure you out of awareness, because it's when you're not in a state of awareness that you have "accidents" and make all the mistakes. Everything can go wrong when you're not aware of what you're doing. That's when you get trapped into taking an instant or reflex action that you don't think about, and that can end up being harmful. If you do this to yourself, the next thing you know, you're in a reactive state to everything around you.

If we look at the world today, we see so many people who are so stressed, so overwhelmed and so depressed. We live in a depressed world. And a depressed world is a world that lacks awareness of its own depression, of its own negative habits. We live in a world where so many people are fat. Why are these people fat? They are fat because they are not aware of all of their bad habits. Their eating is not in tune with the rhythm and biorhythm of their bodies. They're not in tune with their physical needs, with their genetic code, with their biology. They are also not in tune with their families or their environment.

So awareness reconnects us not only to the self, but everything that surrounds us. For example, say you have a sense that something is pressuring you. In order to do something about it, you have to find out what that is. You need to know what is good for you. You have to introspect and investigate what is good for you and what is not good for you. You must ask yourself what it is, in the way you live, that causes your depression. What is it, exactly, that you do that makes you unhealthy?

Sickness or disease (dis-ease) is when you literally disconnect from a feeling of ease; you're not at ease. How many of us are aware that we are not at ease? The majority of us experience moments every day when we're not at ease with the people around us, with the food we eat, with our feelings, or with our own actions. Yet, we keep doing the same thing.

In life you should never do what you're convinced and aware is not good for you. The primal law – the principle of awareness — tells us to do things based on knowing 100% that they correspond with our well-being.

Well-Being

What is your well-being? It's the totality of the Self together with our physical world. Remember, part of the law of awareness is that we are 80% water. The body is made of 80% water. If you look at planet Earth, most of the planet's surface is composed of water, so in one way, we are just a reflection of Mother Earth. The rest of the human body is composed of hydrogen, oxygen and nitrogen, which are three gases, and only one solid component, which is carbon. The molecule of carbon is in the shape of a pyramid — and so is the human body if you sit in the yoga position!

If we go back thousands of years in our evolution, to the time of the Egyptians, we discover that they knew about the body's chemical composition. If you remove the body's water and gas molecules, the one solid element left is carbon. And this is actually how the Egyptians preserved or "mummified" the body, by taking everything out and keeping the solid element of carbon in place. Thousands of years later, we still have the mummies that are perfectly preserved. Being aware that you only have one solid element that is matter (the rest being fluid and gas, which are almost invisible) adds to your perception of "who you are." Clearly, water is a big part of us and represents our emotions, and our emotional system. It shows that water, as an emotional system, dominates us. One sign of that is our ability to cry our tears.

Most of the things that go wrong in our lives are related to our emotions. In order to find balance, we must pay attention to our emotional system and avoid being controlled by our negative emotions.

There are four major negative emotions: anger, hatred, fear and jealousy. Most of us struggle with being in and out of these four emotional states. When you find that you are dominated by any one of these emotions, your state of well-being is affected. When you do things in this world out of anger, you're lacking your own awareness, lacking stability, and are not in your totality. You're missing the "holiness" in you, your connection with the divine; you're missing balance. Therefore, being aware means being in a state of balance; being aware means being in a state of content.

"Heaven is where you'll be
when you're okay right where you are."

—(SourceUnknown)

No wonder one of the oldest civilizations and the oldest religions, Buddhism, talks about Nirvana, the state of joy and happiness. The whole idea today that we need so much meditation and introspection comes from our need to restore this deep happiness, the dream of Nirvana. We can reach a state of Nirvana the more we work with ourselves, and celebrate who we are, and what we are here on Earth to achieve. Being happy with yourself takes you into a state of balance. Having a balanced and stable life comes from awareness.

Strive for awareness in everything you do: in your thoughts and emotions, in how you relate to the people in your life and express yourself, in the words you choose, in how you care for yourself, and in the way you handle your responsibilities. The choices you make each day can lead to a state of health or a state of disease. Being healthy means staying in the light, feeling good, taking care of yourself, and having a good relationship with you. Being unhealthy means "dis-ease" — disconnecting from feeling at ease, being depressed, sick, feeling miserable, and being unbalanced. How can you get to a state of health from there? There is no easy way. Therefore, we need awareness to achieve health and vitality.

To summarize, awareness leads to stability, balance and health, while lack of awareness leads to disease, all kinds of blockages, unhappy and unhealthy behavior, unhealthy patterns, and indirectly, leads to a premature death. The secret of a longer, happier, healthier life is to pay attention every moment — to your thinking, to your actions, and to building positive behaviors and attitudes, shifting all the time towards good habits. It's never too late to change a bad habit, and it's never too late to transform with awareness.

> *Awareness is the basis for transformation,*
> *and transformation is the most*
> *significant law of life.*

HOW TO IMPLEMENT GUIDING PRINCIPLE #1: AWARENESS

Wake up to awareness! Literally! Here are a few tips to raise your awareness and begin to work with it as you awaken in the morning.

WHAT TO DO FIRST THING IN THE MORNING:

Waking up in the morning means waking up to a state of awareness. The first thing you do in the morning is that you become aware — even if it's awareness that it's Monday morning, or that you have a hangover! Waking is awareness. Awareness starts when you wake up in the morning and open your eyes: You become aware of the world around you, and you begin to integrate yourself into your surroundings. The first process of a new day is awareness.

1. Breathe

We recommend that you start each day by taking a deep breath. Open a window if you can, or go out on the porch. If you don't have much time, simply take one mindful breath. As you breathe in, think of breathing in peace, calm, and energy. As you breathe out, release and let go of any stress, fear, or worries you may have.

You can also use breathing as a way to get things into perspective and to connect with the bigger picture. Once you become aware of your own breathing, you will notice that you breathe every few seconds. If you are together with someone else, you may notice that you breathe in a slightly different pattern, but that within the same few seconds you've both taken breaths. If you extend your awareness out into the world, you will understand that within the same very short period of time — just a matter of seconds or minutes — everyone in the world has breathed! All six billion of us! We really are connected at a very basic level.

You can also use your breath to connect to nature. Think of breathing in the clear oxygen that the trees are giving us, and breathing out any toxins. Realize that the air that you breathe has come from the mountains and the oceans. This may be harder to do if you live in the city — and may make you even more aware of environmental issues like clean air!

2. Drink and Eat Mindfully
Start your day with a glass of water. This will rehydrate your body and cleanse toxins accumulated during the night. Drink the water mindfully. Later we suggest that you even drink a glass of soymilk or a cup of tea, or eat a piece of fruit. Think of what you have to accomplish during the day. Establish

peace with the day even if you're going to work and will meet with your difficult boss. Set your mind in positive parameters.

3. "Warm up" Your Body Every Morning (as you would a car)

Have you ever watched a cat waking up? They take their time and stretch. Be like a cat and stretch — become aware of your body before jumping into the business of your day.

4. A Morning Walk/Exercise

Take a walk, even if it's only for a few minutes. When you walk you release vibrations and tension and receive energy in return. Walking is always recommended, not only for exercise, but also as a form of meditation. You can do a walking meditation for as little as three minutes, or for longer at 30-45 minutes.

If possible, plan a short gym/exercise session before breakfast. If you live somewhere where you can go for a walk in a pleasant environment (such as by the beach, in a park, etc.) that's perfect. However, for many people the ideal solution is to invest in a compact, reasonably priced home gym machine. You could also try a fitness ball combined with resistance bands.

Doing exercise first thing in the morning before you eat is highly effective for two reasons. One, you will burn fat because the body is still in its fat-burning mode. This happens because during the night the fuel the body needs to keep your system running (breathing, blood circulation, heart activity, liver, etc.) comes from burning fat. When you wake up in the morning before you eat, the body is still programmed to burn fat. The moment you start eating something, it switches onto burning the food you've eaten. The second reason is that by exercising, you immediately raise your metabolic rate (the rate at which you burn calories) and it will stay up for the rest of the day. However, if your exercise is more on the strenuous side, have a protein drink first. This will protect your muscle mass, yet you will still be burning a significant amount of fat.

5. Break-Fast

Honor yourself by having a healthy breakfast! (In Part II, you'll find some excellent suggestions for a nutritious, delicious breakfast.) Breakfast is very important; you've been fasting the whole night, therefore, breakfast is literally breaking the fast. The first thing you put in your body is important. Make sure you have a balanced breakfast that includes enough protein (we recommend at least 30%), complex carbs (such as whole grain toast), healthy natural fats (like olive oil), fruits and vegetables. A good breakfast will increase your metabolic rate, setting you up for a better day in terms of maintaining or losing weight. It will also stabilize your blood sugar level.

6. How to Start Your Day

Pay attention to how you wake up, the state of being that you implement in yourself. Train yourself to start the day with happy, positive thoughts, such as thoughts of gratitude and appreciation. Focus on what's good in your life.

Be aware of the negative impact of TV news, radio, and newspapers. Try starting your day without reading the paper first thing, and see how your day feels. What are the first images and thoughts you want to put in your mind? In the media world there is a saying, "If it bleeds, it leads." Is that really how you want to start your day? Instead, try reading something inspiring: Look at a beautiful picture or a plant you have at home. You'll find that if you start the day by nourishing your mind, you'll be able to handle the stresses of the day better.

Remember that the next day starts the evening before. Drinking too much wine or caffeine, staying up late watching TV late, everything you do the evening before will affect how your next day starts.

7. Adding 10 Minutes

Many people find waking up, fixing breakfast, and getting themselves and the family off to work or school on time very stressful. Some of us want to stay in bed as long as we possibly can. However, consider waking a little earlier. Those extra 10 minutes "awake" instead of "asleep" could change the whole pace of your day.

8. Claiming Those 10 Minutes

Notice how you can empower yourself when you wake up in the morning and take some time for yourself. For the first few minutes of your day, don't allow anyone or anything to trouble you. Use this time to stay centered within yourself. To some people, and especially to many women, this may sound selfish. It's almost as if we're programmed to put other people and their needs first. However, if you've ever flown and paid attention to the safety information given by the flight attendants, you will know that you are told to put your own oxygen mask on first, and only afterwards to help anyone in your care.

9. The "Right Side" of the Day

Wake up to the idea of awareness, do your meditation walk, have breakfast and program yourself into positive behavior. If you go to work or start your day at home with a positive attitude, knowing that the people at work or those you run into throughout the day might not be your favorite people, according to the universal law of attraction, you will attract more of the good in them and reject their negativity. When we hold onto negative thoughts, we attract people who think negatively into our lives and become entangled in their destructive behaviors and habits. Through the law of awareness we can break through their harmful behavior patterns and get out of the entanglement. Otherwise, we might be stuck in a miserable situation for a long period of time. Awareness is the first step to breaking through.

Summary of Good Morning Tips:
— Drink water, tea, or soy milk.
— Take a deep breath.
— Eat a piece of fruit mindfully.
— Go for a walk for 3 - 30 minutes.
— Do yoga, or tai chi.
— Meditate for one minute or more.
— Meditate in the shower;think of everything that you do well, everything that is positive in your life, everything you're grateful for.

TIPS for AWARENESS THROUGHOUT THE DAY

The Seed and the Oak Tree
Within the tradition of the Kaballah, there is the story

of the seed and the oak tree. Many times it's as if we wake up and all of a sudden there's a great big oak tree growing outside our window. We forget that we ourselves planted the acorn that grew into this oak tree. Nobody just wakes up 100 pounds overweight! They have to be ten pounds overweight first. We need to be aware of what seeds we are planting in our lives.

Activity to Develop Awareness

At any time, when you need to become more aware, you can do this exercise for a few seconds, or a few minutes:

What do you see?

What do you hear?

What do you physically feel?

For example, when you are making a cup of tea in the morning, think about the following questions:

<u>What do you hear?</u>

Hear the sound of the water as you fill the kettle.

Hear the different sounds as the water heats up and boils.

Hear the sounds in the room, the hum of the fridge, the sounds of other people waking up.

Be aware of the sounds that are outside, such as cars, and birds singing.

What do you see?

See the different colors and textures in the room.
Look at the mug.

What do you feel?

Feel the weight of the mug in your hands.
Feel the steam rising to your face.
Feel the taste of the tea/coffee in your mouth.
Feel the effect in your body as the caffeine kicks in!

Meditation Practices

We recommend meditation in any form that you might choose. "Meditation" here means doing whatever you are doing mindfully, with total awareness.

What ALL the following meditation practices have in common is focusing on what you are actually doing in the present moment. You limit your awareness to the activity that you are actually in the process of doing, keeping all your attention on that one activity. Gradually you will be able to allow thoughts to just come and go and not be disturbed by them.

There are many different meditation practices, including:
— Walking Meditation
— Cooking Meditation
— Making Tea/Coffee Meditation
— Eating Meditation

— "One Minute Meditation"
— Wash Your Hands Meditation
— Breathing Meditation
— Compassion Meditation (Meta Bhavana)
— Doing The Dishes Meditation
— Shopping Mediation
— Shaving Meditation

Ritualize

Make your habits a ritual: Rituals can help us by connecting us to something deeper and pulling us into the future.

Let Go and Let God

Think of an organization like Overeaters Anonymous or Alcoholics Anonymous. These organizations have shown the impact of connecting to a higher power (whether it's by meditating, lighting a candle at church, or worshiping at your temple or mosque). They have used the concept of "Let Go and Let God" with amazing results.

Beware! Awareness Thieves!

These are the top 5 "awareness thieves":
1. Alcohol
2. Drugs
3. Stress

4. TV

5. Depression

Making changes in our lives is a matter of establishing good habits and positive rituals. However it's also a matter of _removing_ obstacles that are stopping us.

Mindless eating can be cured with a little attention. Don't watch TV!!

Everything that narrows down your perception steals from your awareness. Everything that widens your perception adds to your awareness. We're only aware of between 2% to 30% of our reality. It would be impossible to live in our world if we were aware of every single thing, every moment of the time. Sometimes we _need_ to do things on "automatic." However, we must make sure that the _right_ things are on automatic.

For example, we all assume that a red traffic light means "stop" and green means "go." If we had to make that decision consciously each time we drive, we'd never get anywhere. However, many of us have bad habits on automatic. We just open the fridge and take whatever's there and "whatever's there" turns out to be not so good for us. We need to program not only ourselves, but also our environment so that it helps and supports us.

Chew!

"Fast food" is not just fast because it's quick to prepare. It's also fast because it's fast to eat. Notice the next time you eat junk food that you really don't have to chew that much. You can pretty much wolf your food down in minutes. But what exactly is this doing to you?

The saliva that is released as you chew food in your mouth is the first stage of digestion. Dr. Gillian McKeith, nutritionist, and program leader for the popular British TV series on eating well, "You Are What You Eat," recommends that you chew until your food has become "liquid." That's the scientific viewpoint. From a spiritual viewpoint, the Buddhists recommend mindfulness as you eat, being aware of the flavors, textures, and of the nutrients being added to your body. Thich Nhat Hanh, a Vietnamese monk living in France and author of many books, recommends 30 chews per mouthful. If you try this, you will probably find that it seems like a rather long time. So our recommendation is that you start with 10 mindful chews per mouthful. Begin to notice which foods need what amount of time to be chewed well.

"We are so far removed from the Earth, our Mother,
that eating is no longer a conscious act.
Nourishment can only be had by awareness,

> *feeding our bodies and souls.*
> *Each thought, each action in the sunlight of*
> *awareness, becomes sacred."*
> — Thich Nhat Hanh, Peace is Every Step

Connected with chewing, here is a weight loss tip: Put your fork down between mouthfuls. Allie was first told this tip when living in Singapore as an 18-year-old. A very beautiful woman in her 60's told her this was her number-one tip for maintaining her weight. It's simple and it works! Try it!

In Sweden, there is even a "Slow Food" movement, started by an Italian immigrant as a reaction to all the fast food.

Awareness and Perception

> *"When you change the way you look at things,*
> *the things you look at change."*
> — Dr. Wayne Dyer

When your perception is opened and you become aware of something you didn't know before, it can really change your life. Here are two examples.

Johnny K's Story
Johnny is a businessman we worked with in Sweden.

One day we took him out to a Malaysian restaurant. We chose the restaurant because it had both great vegetarian (actually vegan) dishes, as well as meat and fish dishes. We all ordered from the menu. Mona and Allie took meat-free and dairy-free options. When the food came, it looked wonderful and we got to talking about food and health. Johnny had high cholesterol and did not feel well from the medication he was on. When we met him again six months later, there was a dramatic change. He looked great and said he felt wonderful! It turned out that he had been going regularly to the Malaysian restaurant and eating his way through the meat-free and dairy-free menu. He also became very interested in how what he ate could affect his health, so he decided to buy some cookbooks and began making healthier food at home as well.

Mona's Story

Some years ago Mona developed an allergy. Nobody could determine exactly what she was allergic to. Her symptoms were a build-up of mucus and difficulty breathing. Her doctor prescribed a cortisone spray and other medications to alleviate the symptoms. Then, from several different sources, she discovered that giving up milk products could help. One included a TV interview with Celine Dion. She mentioned how, during the year she took off from singing, she could eat cheese again. Normally, she avoided milk products. Many actors and singers apparently avoid milk and milk products before a performance. Mona also read in the Swedish papers how children who were very susceptible to ear infections became much healthier when they stopped taking milk products. Eating a lot of meat-free foods, cheese was often the "protein" option for Mona. By the third time she heard the same information about cheese, she thought, "Well, I might as well try giving it up." She stopped eating dairy products, and within 48 hours her breathing was better! She could hardly believe it. Some months later when Mona went to her ear, nose and throat specialist for a checkup, he said, "I see you are using your cortisone regularly!" He didn't seem to believe her when she told him how she cut out dairy products. A few months later, as an added bonus to alleviating her allergy and sinus symptoms, her "bad" cholesterol level dropped by 50%!

Chapter Two:

Guiding Principle #2: Be Proactive
Avoid Reactivity

The first principle of awareness leads to the second law. Once you're aware of yourself and the world around, you can choose either constructive behavior or destructive behavior towards yourself. We call the second guiding principle *the principle of being proactive,* because being proactive is a positive law; it creates a positive state of being. It's the law that governs making positive choices for yourself, and with awareness, knowing what you have to do. We always have choices: We have the choice to take things one way or another. So being proactive means being creatively constructive towards yourself, and finding new avenues to pursue. One thing is certain: You must put your willpower to work. Being proactive means using your willpower to break any negative tendencies that exist within you, or any temptation in the world around you. You don't have to be reactive; you can choose to be proactive.

These are ancient teachings. Being proactive is what the Kaballah teaches us — to be proactive toward our surroundings, and not reactive. The world we live in has a constant tendency towards reaction. Most of the time when you react to the world around you, that reaction is negative. But if you stop to analyze your reaction in a positive way and invert it, you can benefit from what happens in the outside world, rather than feeling victimized by it. The world is always testing us. Being proactive means testing yourself and making better choices. It's extremely important to teach yourself to become proactive and make positive choices. These choices begin with what you eat, how you choose to eat, when and where you eat, how much time you give yourself to relax, and how you start a new day.

Resisting Temptation

"Resisting" is a significant concept in being proactive. Temptation surrounds us all the time — the temptation of going with the flow of our daily routine or just with the flow of life, which often may not be constructive. We frequently do things without analyzing, without introspection, without thinking. Every day we do many things "automatically." That's the problem — for instance, we don't consider whether or not something is good for us to eat, or we don't think about giving ourselves enough time for relaxation. We just pretend we don't have time. The Kaballah also teaches us we must often resist an urge in order to be in control. Being in control in a good way — by taking charge and tuning in to the spiritual you — makes you stronger. This kind of resistance gives you strength, the same way "resistance training" with weights at the gym strengthens your muscles. Resistance empowers you by helping your life to flow. You become so powerful; you give yourself the right to say no to any temptation, and you feel good about that "no." You heal your weaknesses when you apply this Kaballistic law of resisting everything around you that might be harmful to you.

Once you combine your awareness of what's not healthy for you with the strength of resistance, you've achieved the second law. By putting the first two guiding principles together, you can build something which, from that day on, is not going to be a problem. The moment you resist, you shift your frequency, and from that day forward it will be easier to integrate the positive tools and constructive patterns into your life.

We're not born with good behavioral patterns, we have to create them; everything comes by creation. Life is our creation. Resistance is a tool that can create the positive you in a positive environment. Part of the power of resistance comes from your belief in your right to not be like everyone else. Resisting some types of food, resisting addiction, resisting smoking, resisting eating in front of the TV, and resisting eating in the movie theater, are all examples of resisting behaviors that have become like a national habit, a national pattern. These are things that you do because everyone else does, and you feel like you have to "go along" with everybody. The principle of resistance demonstrates how you can choose differently — to not be like everyone else. You don't have to drink just because your father drinks. You don't have to engage in destructive habits just because it's in your family or in your environment. It's your responsibility to be aware of what is healthy and what is harmful for you.

This book can help you to be responsible for you, to build "you" and to be clear about building a healthy life. It also offers some of the ancient teachings such as, for example, the Kaballistic principle of resistance, that you may not have considered before as being beneficial to your well-being.

We, as a society, have fallen into a pattern of bad habits. When you look at our world today, you see a fast-food restaurant on almost every street corner. Many people are consuming all sorts of junk food because that's what everybody else does. So this book teaches how to not be like everybody else, to keep from falling into harmful social patterns. You have the right to choose for yourself. You have the right to resist, the right to reject, the right to create, to be proactive. You have the right to construct, you have the right to your own self, to your well-being.

Your well-being has to do with what is good for you, and not necessarily what is good for another. What is good for you is your own good. You don't have to compare yourself with anyone else. Using the principle of being proactive, you learn not to compare yourself with others. When you stop comparing, you start being yourself. Then you can begin to resist temptation, and to become proactive at building the healthy you.

HOW TO IMPLEMENT GUIDING PRINCIPLE #2: BE PROACTIVE

Think about each of the following:

You need to think about these questions when you eat...

> *What?*
> *When?*
> *Where?*
> *How Much?*
> *Why?*
> *With Whom?*
> *How?*
> *How Often?*

Many people say, "It's just the way I am!" And in a way that's true. It _is_ the way you are — until you decide to change.

Resist the "Big Four" Foods to Say No To:

The White Stuff — White, processed, refined carbohydrates such as white flour

Include more complex carbohydrates, i.e., the brown stuff, such as brown rice. Ask for brown rice in restaurants, especially in Asian restaurants. You'll be surprised how often they have it! Ask for whole wheat pasta in Italian restaurants. Look for whole grain alternatives in the

supermarket. These are also known as the "good" carbs. Complex, whole grain carbs are also lower on the GI index, which means they will keep you feeling fuller longer, and help prevent blood sugar swings.

Sugar — White, refined sugar
Use brown sugar, Demerara sugar, or other natural sweeteners such as organic maple syrup, honey, and fruit. Check the sugar content on food labels e.g., cereal, yogurt, bread, baked beans, and even "health" products like protein bars and protein drinks.

Salt — White, refined salt
Use herb salt, or natural sea salt in moderation. Use herbs and spices in cooking to achieve more flavors.

Saturated Fat — the "bad" fat from dairy products and meat
Include healthier alternatives: "better dairy" like cottage cheese, fresh goat's cheese, mozzarella, feta cheese; also egg white omelets.

Think, for example, about the Mediterranean diet where small amounts of dairy are used. According to European studies, Greeks have consistently come out on top in terms of healthy eating. Also in China, Japan and Southeast Asia where there is traditionally no dairy in their diets, fewer people suffer from food-related disorders.

It's an Acquired Taste

For example, genetically, as a survival mechanism, we are wired to recoil from things that taste bitter or have a burning sensation. In spite of that, hundreds of millions of people all over the world love chili! Many more learn to enjoy hot food when they travel to other countries or try different restaurants. This fact has aroused the interest of researchers: Are we wired differently so that, for example, some people can take chili and others can't? Research has not found any significant difference in chili eaters and others.

What does happen is that our brains are able to override what our instincts are signaling is wrong for us. For example, many people are afraid of public speaking and yet they get up and make their presentations anyway. Many people overcome their natural fear of falling and enjoy the thrill of bungee jumping, or a rollercoaster. In the same way, we can override what our brains are telling us about the possible dangers of food that gives us a burning sensation, and instead learn to savor that very sensation. Therefore, get into new foods like, for example, tofu, Quorn, or quinoa.

Get into Action

Energy is constantly moving. It is not natural for us

to be sedentary for long periods of time. Get your energy moving in any way you can. This is the energy that is also called "ki" and "chi" in Asia. Move around or stand up and stretch every half hour. Set a timer to remind you.

The three G's

Any time you're feeling a little down and stuck, try this simple formula:

Get up!

Get dressed!

Get out!

"Just do it!"

The Nike slogan is an excellent reminder. Sometimes it's better not to look before you leap. Sometimes you need to just get moving and things will happen to you. The Chinese have a saying: "If you spend too long deciding on the next step, you will spend your life standing on one leg!" So keep yourself active: Start a movement/activity diary to keep track of how well you're doing.

Chapter Three:

Guiding Principle #3: Find Balance
See the Bigger Picture

Finding our balance is about seeing life in the big picture. Life is not only about what you do and what you think. It is the totality of everything that you affect and that affects you: from your thinking to your actions, to how you express yourself, to your energy and the frequencies you hold, to the people in your life. That's how to see life as a totality.

Many times we are so focused on where we're going that we miss the bigger picture. We all want to be healthy, happy and centered, moving toward our goals and dreams, but sometimes we get tunnel vision. We narrow the idea of balance and stability, and what it means to take care of ourselves properly. Living a good life definitely means taking care of yourself. Living a good life definitely means reaching a state of happiness. But the problem comes when you fail to connect your thinking with your action, or your action doesn't reflect what you're thinking. When that happens, you can miss something significant in your daily routine. That's when you're missing the bigger picture.

It's not always easy to see the bigger picture because you have to connect with all your available resources. You have to integrate yourself into the world, the universe. Seeing the bigger picture goes hand-in-hand with the balance of life. The balance of life requires stability. Our body is made of two forces: yin and yang, the minus and the plus. In order to create a stable totality, we must put the two parts together.

Having a good life means having good eating habits, sleeping well, exercising, and enjoying a good career and good relationships. The bigger picture involves being harmonious in all our relationships. Our relationships with others are equally important as being happy in our private lives or our careers. If something is missing somewhere in the link of this totality, the chain is broken and we are not happy. When people are not happy that gets reflected in their habits. Bad habits are always associated with emotions and stem from overwhelming feelings. As I mentioned earlier, it's difficult to maintain balance and stability when your emotions are pulling you off course. The people you see around you that are overweight or too skinny, or even anorexic, are struggling to maintain balance. Their struggles have a lot to do with what they are feeling about themselves, and the state of their emotions.

Our emotional system plays a big part in our ability to maintain stability and balance. When your emotions are in place, your relationships are in place. Only then do you have the strength and stability to program your life.

Life is actually programmed by us. What we think, we become. How we behave, and the image we project in the world, is the result of our outlook on life. When you are in emotional balance, you will be able to eat properly, integrate exercise into your life, sleep well, and relax. People who have nightmares and cannot sleep are also suffering from emotional imbalances. How those people keep balance, I don't know! It's almost impossible to reach a state of balance when you're dominated by fear, or a phobia, or any other strong emotional imbalance.

Although I'm a psychologist, I don't really believe in the practice of prescribing drugs in order to deal with emotional imbalance. Almost every other person that goes to a psychiatrist receives a prescription for drugs. Because these prescriptions seem to go on forever, they create other addictions, and make the person believe that they have a problem that cannot be cured. As a result, people live with the belief that their problem has taken control of their lives, and that they'll never be able to fix it, when in fact we can fix everything. We can bring everything back to balance — the body, the mind and the soul — no matter what issues might surface at a certain stage of evolution. The very reason these issues surface is for them to be healed.

Going through life is like being on a roller coaster! Life is not perfect. Life brings us all kinds of episodes and turning points. These are initiations and themes of life that we have to go through to achieve wholeness. Going through the themes of life with serenity allows us to maintain control. Keeping balance also requires control. If you want to keep your life stable and in balance, then you must learn to be in control of your emotions, your actions, and everything you do to others, in addition to what you do to yourself.

Being Organized

You have to be organized, because if you're not, life takes you all over the place, and you won't feel centered. Being centered means being organized. As we mentioned before, once you wake up in the morning and become aware, you can use that awareness to center things in your life by organizing what you eat, when you exercise, what time you go to sleep. You don't have to become a machine, but we live in a world of chronology, and things have to be placed in time. The more you organize your day to have your meals at the same time, and sleep at the same time, the more balance you will bring into your life.

But in the crazy technological world we are living in, sometimes it's impossible to stay organized. If, for instance, you rely on going to work on the bus or train, and there happens to be a delay, then you get to work and your boss screams at you, that throws off your whole day. That's just one example of how easily life can take you out of your emotional balance. You plan to have a meal, but cannot go because there's something else you have to show up for. We live in a fast-paced society, in a world that is pressuring us. When the world applies pressure, we apply pressure to ourselves. And when we pressure ourselves, we get out of balance. If you walk in the street for ten minutes, you seldom see people who look relaxed and balanced and who know what they're doing with their lives.

So having balance means being aware of what you're doing to yourself, knowing every moment. It all comes down to awareness, to reach this state of stability. Life must have stability. Without stability, life is chaos. You don't want to live in chaos, because then your body goes out of control: You cannot sleep well, you become addicted to drugs and pills, and you will believe that you're sick.

The world we live in relies on belief systems, and that's what we need to work on as a society, as a totality, as a collective consciousness. When we change our beliefs, we change our lives. If we begin with the belief that we are designed to be in balance, then that's what we'll achieve: that we are designed to be here on Earth and have the ability to cope with the challenges that come our way.

HOW TO IMPLEMENT GUIDING PRINCIPLE #3: FIND BALANCE

Moderation in All Things, and All Things in Moderation

More or less everyone has heard this from parents or grandparents, and there is certainly a lot of wisdom in these words! You can eat or do more or less anything you want — some of the time. The key is: What are the things you are doing on a regular basis? What are the habits and rituals of your life? For example, in Sweden, there is a special Lent bun called a "semla." It is sold traditionally during Lent. The "semla" is made of a sweet bun, with a marzipan and fresh cream filling. If you are familiar with the points system of Weight Watchers, one "semla" is practically all your points for an entire day! At the same time, they are rather delicious. The solution? Decide to just have one or two during the "semla season." This goes for anything else, too — chocolate bars, chips, French fries, pizza, etc. Have anything you want — sometimes. But make your regular habits healthy.

Staying Flexible – Be Like the Bamboo

Bamboo is a strong and flexible tree. It bends in a storm, but rarely breaks. We can set our goal to be flexible like that. If we have created a ritual to start our day with a walk, and then one day we don't have time, we need to make sure that that does not ruin our equilibrium. We need to be inclusive in our thinking. To be a person who generally eats nourishing, healthy food and enjoys cream cake sometimes.

Avoid Being Extreme

Don't be extreme in being vegetarian or vegan, but also don't be extreme as a meat eater. Don't be extreme as an exerciser, but don't sit on the sofa all day every day, either. Give food, exercise, sleep and rest the right place in your life. And make sure your emotions are as stable as possible. Then moderation comes naturally.

In her book *Why People Don't Heal And How They Can*, Caroline Myss gives the example of a young man who is into very healthy living, and even grows his own organic food. However, one day he learns he has contracted a form of cancer. He is very bitter and cannot understand why, with his healthy lifestyle, he got sick. Eventually he died. Somewhere in his life he was out of balance, and not making choices out of joy.

The Power of Full Engagement

Imagine life as series of sprints, not a marathon. A healthy EKG reading is an oscillating line, not a flat line. To stay healthy and happy, we need to build balance and variety into our lives. In their book

The Power of Full Engagement, Jim Loehr and Tony Schwartz claim that the problem is not speed and stress. On the contrary, we benefit from the "power of full engagement." However, the problem is that, as a culture, we do not recognize the vital need for recovering from stress. A cellular phone "dies" when its battery runs out and has to be recharged. It is exactly the same for us humans, only most of the time we keep going anyway, even though our "batteries" have run out.

Other Practical Tips on How to Achieve More Balance:

1. Do simple ki aikido exercises (can be applied to any physical exercises). E.g., Stand, sit, walk with "ki", even speak with "ki" "Ki" — or "chi"— refers to the Asian concept of "keeping one point." This point is located a few inches below your navel. It is also the point of balance that dancers, horse-riders and singers learn to focus on. This balances you and aligns you along your natural gravity line. Any form of martial art, Tai Chi, yoga, or even sports generally, will help you find this point naturally and will give you more balance. If you'd like to know more about this, read the book *Ki in Daily Life* by Koichi Tohei.
2. Swim for balance. When we swim, all the muscles

of the body are involved, and the body works as one unit.

3. Explore how you can work with a fitness ball. This is a playful activity that will give you joy and improve your balance into the bargain.

4. Do a one-minute meditation (e.g., read the *book The One-Minute Meditator* for more ideas).

5. Take "time-out" — a mini-break — to regain balance.

6. Regain mental balance and stability by restoring your "GABA." "GABA" is a signal substance in the brain that cannot function properly without long periods of sobriety. Three months without drinking alcohol is required to reset the GABA back to normal. (This is based on recent Swedish research quoted in *Bolaget* Magazine, in an article entitled, "What Schnapses Does To Your Synapses.") However, even a "white," i.e., alcohol-free week, will help.

Chapter Four:

Guiding Principle #4: Seek Joy
Slow Down and Enjoy the Ride

At the heart of this book is in fact its spiritual component. We not only have to eat right, exercise regularly, know which exercises are good for us, and when to sleep and be perfectly organized in our "program" of daily life, but we also have to add a spiritual component. That component is the key to joy, to being all of this and maintaining a happy mood. The more you integrate the spiritual component in your life, the easier it becomes to break negative habits. Otherwise, there's so much ego and resistance to transformation. Joy is a part of your spiritual connection and well-being. The more joy you experience, the easier everything becomes, and the more spiritual you become.

When I go to the gym myself, what I see at times are people who are there because they feel they have to go. Their minds are not there; they are like robots. They feel that they have to use all those machines, but there is no pleasure in it for them anymore — they have lost the pleasure of what they are doing for themselves. In restaurants, I see people who come out to eat, but have to eat a specific kind of food, and they're so stuck and rigid in their ways that they don't enjoy themselves. Life is for enjoyment. Learn to enjoy things that are good for you, things that lead to positive outcomes. That's how you program your environment for success.

Bringing wholeness to your life is not just about willpower. You have to create a structure in your life that supports you. Never do things in a narrow way, that's becoming a fundamentalist. Fundamentalism in any form is a narrow, orthodox way of looking at the world. Unfortunately, every religion in the world has some aspect of this — a narrow understanding — even in its concept of God. For example, some religions have an angry God.

At this stage in our evolution, we have to get beyond the philosophy and concepts that tell us to be rigid in the way we do things. Everything has to come with joy, because our stability is connected to doing things with pleasure. Eat with pleasure, exercise with pleasure, be happy when you go to sleep, remember your dreams with joy, be surrounded by family and friends, enjoy outdoor activities, go swimming, go fishing. Everything that is part of your relaxation is part of the bigger picture and should lead to joy. If we focus on joy, the bigger picture becomes everything that pleases you. Never overdo anything; do everything in moderation, including exercise. Never be compulsive in anything you do, because compulsive behavior can easily take over and steal all your joy.

Motivating with Joy

When you motivate yourself, motivate yourself knowing that you have to limit your actions, limit your exercise, and not overdo anything. That's the key to reaching stability, the key to balance, and the key to joy. Why pursue just one thing, one narrow way, when you can enjoy the abundance of the universe? In order to experience joy, you need to experience the totality of your life. Some people exercise, but they eat badly; some people eat well, but don't exercise. Others do eat well and exercise but cannot sleep because of all of their problems — with their mother-in-law, or God knows whom!

There are all of these components that you have to consider when you wake up in the morning. Every single day of your life, you have to think about relationships. That is one of the keys to being more joyful. Exercise is also one of the keys. Eating well is another. Going outdoors is a key. Life indoors can be like a prison. Go out! Even in prison they let you out! Do things for the pleasure of doing them, not like a machine because you're programmed. Instead, associate your program with joy.

Your first priority should be joy. When you wake up, say thank you for being alive, say "I'm glad for another beautiful day! I enjoy the birds singing; I enjoy the sun; I enjoy the green grass and trees. I enjoy every season, and I celebrate!" Celebrating life brings emotional stability. When the mind is stable and in control, you can reach a state of joy and balance. When you have joy, balance is easy to achieve. When you're joyful and balanced, you can put many other things on your program. It's up to joy — and joy in life is up to you. But some guidance always helps.

HOW TO IMPLEMENT GUIDING PRINCIPLE #4: SEEK JOY

Joy and stress cancel out each other. If you're experiencing stress, you're not experiencing joy. If you're not experiencing joy, perhaps you're too stressed. In addition, the stress hormone, cortisol, locks excess fat in place in the belly area, which is exactly where you least want it for your health. All the time-saving devices available to us haven't actually saved us time. Many people are more stressed than ever. We're wired for joy and happiness. According to recent brain research, it seems that the "pursuit of happiness" is wired into our brains. We can use this knowledge in creating better lives for ourselves. For example, start creating — at least once a day — an environment where the enjoyment of eating can take center stage. We suggest going to a nice restaurant and being served wholesome, delicious food that you have time to savor.

Variety is the Spice of Life

The function of dopamine in our brains is to make it joyful for us to try new things. However, many of us get stuck in a rut, and then are afraid of doing something new. Try this simple tip: Do something new each day. Something "new" can also be something you haven't done in a long while, so that it feels new. For example: Go to work a different way; wear a blouse you haven't worn for a long time; eat lunch out if you usually just sit at your desk; try a new food. Joy is in the details. Become more aware of what you are doing and the world around you. Try the "What do you see/hear/feel?" exercise (from Chapter One).

Morning and Evening Rituals; Gratitude Journal

Try the following:

Gratitude Journal:

At the end of the day, write five things that you are grateful for. Try to make it specific things, rather than general. For instance, "I'm grateful for the man who opened the door for me," rather than "I'm grateful for kind people." This will help you to find joy in the details. You will find yourself looking for things you can be grateful for. If you don't want to write, you can just go through these things in your head before you go to sleep.

Just One Thing:

What is the one thing you're happiest about today? Or what is the one thing that has meant the most today?

Try these "Morning" and "Evening" questions when you go to sleep and when you wake up, or make up your own questions:

Morning questions:

Who loves me? And whom do I love?

What am I happy about in my life in this moment?

What am I excited about in my life in this moment?

What am I proud of in my life in this moment?

Evening questions:

What have I given or shared today?

What have I learned today?

How can I use this day as an investment for the future?

What am I most grateful for today?

Find Joy in New Things

Make a new connection.

For some people, "healthy" has positive connotations: feeling well, looking good, etc. But for some, the word "healthy" has negative connotations: deprivation, strict rules, boring food, not eating anything they like. So how do you create a new connection? How do you "buzz" on what you want to feel like: joy, happiness, and peace. If you are "healthy", what is FEELING healthy for you? Is it joy?, Satisfaction?, Happiness?, Calm?

Some people say, "Well, it's joyful for me to eat a whole candy bar," or "It's joyful for me to eat a huge steak with French fries," or "It's joyful for me to eat a doughnut." Think more deeply: Is it really joyful to be overweight? Is it really joyful to know that you are putting chemicals or bad cholesterol into your body? Be willing to change the way you think about food. Find joy in delicious whole foods and returning to more natural foods.

Eat With Joy!

Some women on a first date will hardly eat anything, as if there's something wrong with the natural process of eating, as if we're afraid of losing control in the presence of food. What can we learn from men about eating? Men tend to eat with more pleasure and less guilt. They don't agonize afterwards; they go the gym instead!

Humor

Humor is a skill. Finding what's funny is a skill. Being able to tell a funny story is a skill. You need to practice. Eastern European cultures are much better at this than the Western world. Go through your day looking for funny things. Don't laugh at others in an unkind way, just look for the humor in everyday situations.

Making Joyful Choices

Be conscious of what you put in your mind, the kind of people you surround yourself with or attract into your life:

— Actively choose what TV programs you watch,

what movies you go to.

— Avoid TV news and newspapers.

— Practice the "Let Go and Let God" technique when other people try to drag you into their personal dramas.

— Choose the people you really want to be with, and ask yourself, "Are these real friends?"

Connect with Others and Be Generous

In his book *The Power of Intention,* Wayne Dyer has an interesting perspective on this. One of his main points, supported by scientific findings, is how serotonin levels are affected positively by our connection to others, by our kindness and generosity. More on this in the next chapter on Togetherness.

Chapter Five:

Guiding Principle #5: Treasure Togetherness
Cultivate Connection and Generosity

Togetherness, connection, love, generosity, and gratitude — these are the most beautiful aspects of creating joy and stability. Food is given to us by God. If you look at this beautiful world we live in, it's definitely the creation of a Divine energy. We, too, are divine and everything that we touch should be divine; everything that we do should be constructive and not destructive. This is the principle of life and survival.

What we're missing in the world today, in the world of the computer, is connection. We're disconnected from each other. Many people that I see in my practice in Manhattan just go home alone. They never have time to talk to other people face to face. They correspond only through text messages and email. The real genuine human contact is lost. The idea of those beautiful family gatherings of the past is lost.

And once you begin to lose your sense of connection that leads to isolation and depression.

So if you want to celebrate the gift of God, such as food, why not celebrate it together? How wonderful it is to be invited somewhere and sit with someone at their table and just share feelings, emotions, thoughts, as you share the beautiful food. Food should hardly ever be eaten alone. Because it is the gift of God, food should be a celebration between people. You eat differently when you are surrounded by other people, when you feel the warmth and the joy of the human connection; fun and humor also add to the joy and the celebration.

Almost any cookbook that you find will show pictures of people together, gathered around a table. Think of how successful Jamie Oliver, *"The Naked Cook,"* has been. He always suggests cooking for people, even if it's just one friend coming around. He always shows the connection between food, sharing with others, and having fun.

Think of Jesus and the Last Supper. Many stories about Jesus have to do with sharing food, and the symbolism of food, of being fed, the bread and fish, and breaking bread with someone.

We recommend that when you think of food, or any other activities you enjoy, try to do as many of those as possible with other people, even meditation. Meditation is quite special and powerful when practiced in a group. Don't isolate yourself and become stuck in the habit of eating alone; when you eat alone, you will think of all your issues. Eat with other people so that you can get out of yourself. This will help put your problems in perspective, and reduce your ego and self-centeredness. It's also a way to break your routine.

Be aware of what has become part of your "routine," and make your routines more like positive rituals rather than straightjackets of mechanical repetition. For example, I know of a woman who's lonely. Every single day of her life she stays alone in her house, and eats by herself. How sad and depressing and demoralizing this is. At least some of our daily activities should be done with other people. Even if you don't have a partner, invite your friends in to join you. Friendship is part of balance and stability, and also part of the law of togetherness and sharing love.

When God created the world, it began with two to share love. You cannot share love by yourself. A lot of people in this society have dogs, cats or other pets and use them to replace human love, because they need love. While pets are wonderful, they cannot replace human love.

Gratitude and Generosity

Be grateful for your meals, your health, and every breath that you take. Be generous with food: it's good to give food away. Give food to people, give energy to others, give advice to others, and give clothing to others. Giving is receiving. Give something to beggars and to old people, even if it's just a blessing. Wherever you go, bring a small gift, even if it's a card or a flower. Giving is a symbol of expressing, and is the most beautiful way of expressing compassion and love.

Inviting People In

The most wonderful moments in a year include traditional celebrations such as Thanksgiving, Christmas, and Chanukah, when people gather together. Food becomes the central attraction. But why wait for some holiday or occasion to celebrate? We can celebrate life all the time through togetherness, by inviting friends and cousins in from who knows where, or inviting people even from other parts of the world. The more we surround ourselves with people, the better life gets.

Parties and Weddings

People love parties, but the greatest celebration of all for many people is celebrating a wedding. What is a wedding all about, but coming together in front of the world, before a table where there's food. Celebrating life definitely means sharing food. It's one of the fundamental elements of celebration. Every culture adds its own meanings. In China, they associate the word "party" with food, but not alcohol; while in Sweden, the word "party" means a lot of alcohol.

Look at every meal as an opportunity to include more fun, more joy, and more spiritual aspects in your life. The more you do this within a year, the happier you'll become, because this book is about, over and over again, being happy. And how are you going to be happy if you don't know how to share yourself with others? If you don't know how to share happiness and compassion, if you don't know love, if you don't know how to give and don't understand generosity, if you don't know how to share a meal with someone else, then you are lacking the most fundamental principles of healthy, happy living, and of feeling whole and spiritual.

If you apply these simple principles, you will find each day your life will become easier, balanced and free. You will free yourself from all the narrow concepts of living and open to a much larger picture of life. Togetherness goes hand-in-hand with love and gratitude, and these should be expressed at every meal, every moment, when you exercise, every moment that you share yourself with other people. The more you share your life with others, the better and healthier your life will be.

HOW TO INTEGRATE
PRINCIPLE #5: TREASURE TOGETHERNESS

"In music, in the sea, in a flower, in a leaf, in an act of kindness…I see what people call God in all these things."
— Pablo Casals

Giving and Our Brains

Recent brain research shows that, with giving and receiving, the immune system actually improves, in the person giving and in the person receiving. So in that sense, giving IS receiving! And, surprisingly enough, even a third-party observer benefits. Think of Mother Theresa, and Princess Diana: Watching the way they were in the world gave us a sense of well-being and inspired us. A recent example is Oprah Winfrey. Millions of people around the world are constantly being inspired by her to live better lives, to do good and to give to others.

The Soap Opera of Real Life!

Instead of watching a TV soap opera about imaginary lives, get involved in "soap operas" from the real world. Truth is more amazing than fiction, so take the opportunity to connect and help someone in need, even if it's just by listening. When we "just listen" without judgment, we hold a space that can bring ease to what is being spoken. Make a call, or see family and friends; show an interest in someone's life.

Managing Conflicts and Improving Relationships

Maybe you're thinking, "Well, I love all this ideal "white-picket scenario," and big happy families gathered around the table, but that's just not the way it is with my family." Here are some tips on conflict resolution in order to encourage connection and togetherness with family, friends, and co-workers:

1. Giving gifts helps; they're the modern equivalent of an olive branch!
2. Apologizing doesn't cost anything and often breaks a negative, downward spiral of interaction.
3. Any act of kindness increases your serotonin level.
4. More frequency of contact rather than less helps when there is a conflict, although this is "counter-instinctive." Of course, if emotions are running high, wait for them to subside somewhat first, otherwise you'll just get more of the same. Also try doing something different, like going out to a restaurant rather than staying at home.
5. You don't necessarily have to talk about everything and "work it out." You might never understand! "We tried to talk it over, but the words got in the way," was a line in a Karen Carpenter song. Sometimes

it's just better to go on, acknowledging that you do want this connection in some way. Find a "zone of possible agreement."

6. Love is a verb. Just saying "I love you" doesn't mean much. Do something loving. Show loving behavior in your concrete actions.

7. Be unconditionally constructive: Do what's good for you and the relationship. Train yourself to respect differences. Respect how both you and the other party are different from each other.

8. Always remember to include yourself in the people you love!

9. Learn "Meta bhavana," a Buddhist meditation practice, a way of thinking of yourself and others with compassion

10. Light a candle and "Let go and let God."

"People come into your life for a reason, for a season, for a lifetime. Sometimes they don't come to stay."

— Iyanla Vanzant

Learn to let go and move on.

We're Wired For Togetherness!

Your brain is wired for face-to-face contact. We can use this information in improving our relationships. For example, when you just send an email, the other person tries to interpret your tone of voice, your look, and your intentions. "Smilies" help but they are often not enough. The next best is a phone call and the best of all is actually getting together. Then the emotional part of your brain, the mammal brain, will give you a better chance at establishing an improved connection. Otherwise, the connection remains only on the level of words, where most misunderstandings occur.

Time Alone

However, as with all the guiding principles, moderation is the key and alone time is also important! In this era of cellular phones ringing all over the place, it is more important than every to carve out a silent space for yourself. Try to do this on a daily basis, even if it's only for a few minutes.

Tips for Togetherness at The Table

> *"Eating on the run is a missed opportunity to connect with another human being."*
> — Danny Meyer, restaurateur and owner
> of eight NYC restaurants
> (*O Magazine*, August 2005)

Here are some more tips specifically aimed at the idea of eating together:

1. Gather around food and say a prayer of gratitude for the people in your life and the food on

your table. Be grateful to all the people who've contributed to putting the food on your table: the farmers, those who transported the food, those who sell it, the person who has prepared it, the person who is serving it, and so on.

2. Say grace.

3. The Unexpected Guest: There is an Eastern European tradition of setting a place for the "unexpected guest."

4. Remember to toast absent friends.

5. Every meal is a chance to include more spirituality in your life. Even for breakfast, put a flower on the table. Act in such a way that you demonstrate how you take things in your life with gratitude, rather than for granted. We don't need to feel guilty that we so easily can fill our stomachs; however, we do need to feel grateful. Far from being our enemy, food can be our friend and keep us grounded in every day (IF we are eating the right food).

6. Make mealtimes a moment of mindfulness and connectedness: Turn off the TV!

Intention

> *"Intention isn't necessarily something I do,*
> *but something I connect to."*
>
> — Dr. Wayne Dwyer

Our source is spirit — it is something other than the physical. How rusty is your connection to the spiritual and to other people? What could you do today to be more connected? Mealtimes, for example, offer us a great opportunity for a moment of connectedness.

Tithing

One way to feel connected is to give to others. An old tradition is the idea of tithing, which is giving away 10% of your income. If you read the papers or see the news, you will certainly be aware of so many good causes to give to, it can feel overwhelming. One suggestion is to choose one or two causes that you want to support. What is closest to your heart? Giving to the environment? To children? To emergency work? To disaster relief? To young musicians? To your local school or church?

A Few More Simple Tips on Togetherness:

1. Call at least one friend every day.
2. Be more spontaneous: Don't overload your schedule with big planned things like dinners and celebrations. Just ask someone to come around for coffee, or suggest you go there for just half an hour to see them and give them a hug.
3. Make sure you have time to stop and chat to a neighbor or someone else in the community.

Give yourself some extra time so that you can stop and ask how they are.

Chapter Six:

Guiding Principle #6: Return to Mother Nature
Eat Real Food and Move Your Body

Return to Nature

The purpose of this book is to guide people back to the source of our physical survival, the source of real food — Mother Nature. Eating from nature is how we originally survived. Only in our recent history have we begun to process our foods, and as a result, we've changed almost everything that Mother Nature generated and intended for our survival. Eating from Mother Nature makes perfect sense. Everything from nature is alive: it's colorful, it's unaltered, it provides us with the perfect ingredients — the right vitamins, minerals and nutrients that we need to survive. They occur naturally in the world around us.

Color

The world we live in is full of color. We are colorful people and should eat colorful things. Vegetables and fruit come in yellow, golden, green, orange,

red, even purple and blue. All of the produce that
nature so generously offers us is in accordance
with the frequencies of the universe. In the 18th
century, scientists realized that the color white
doesn't really exist. If you take white light and put
it through a spectrum, it divides into seven colors,
which correspond exactly with the seven elements,
the mystical number of 7, seven days of the week,
seven musical notes, and seven frequencies in the
human body.

The seven vibrations of the white light are red,
orange, yellow, green, blue, indigo, and violet.
These frequencies can be translated into what
ancient cultures called the seven points of energy,
the so-called chakra points. We believe that if you
want to achieve a healthy life, you must make sure
that your chakra points are balanced. When your
chakras are balanced, the frequencies of energy flow
through you naturally. When one chakra becomes
blocked, its color frequency stops flowing and we
can develop a problem in that particular part of the
body. For instance, if you have a problem related to
expressing love, the heart chakra — which vibrates
at the green frequency — may be closed or blocked.
One consequence of a having a blocked heart chakra
might be a heart attack. Another example would
be that if you have problems expressing yourself,

or standing up for yourself, you could develop a problem in the throat area, the blue frequency. As a result, you might develop throat cancer or problems with breathing. Every problem that develops in your physical body is related to these points of energy. So the seven frequencies, the seven colors, are actually a part of our nature. If you look at all the fruits and vegetables, as I mentioned before, they also reflect all the rays in the color spectrum.

Working with Food and Color

The color of a food tells you a lot about what it can do for you. For example, if you have high blood pressure, you need to avoid the color red, because red is associated with high blood pressure. Try to eat something that's more green or yellow. Vitamin C relates to the color yellow, so if you lack vitamin C in your body, try to eat things that are yellow or gold or orange, because yellowish, golden colored fruits and vegetables are naturally high in vitamin C.

If you look at the color of the food you eat, each holds a different frequency, with red being the highest frequency, and violet being the lowest frequency. Relating that to the chakra points in the body, the root chakra, at the base of the spine is red, and the crown chakra, at the top of the head, is violet. Violet is the lowest frequency and the most spiritual color. Because it's at the top of the head, when you concentrate, you generate that frequency. We actually generate colors all the time. If you think of modern aura photography, it shows that around our physical bodies is an aura that reflects the color frequency that we give off.

"Everything in life strives for color"
— Goethe

Color and Emotions

We also can associate color with emotions. For example, the color red represents anger. So avoid red meat if you are angry. Eat more green (the color of the heart chakra) instead, such as vegetables and salads. The color violet represents calm and spirituality, and blue represents serenity and acceptance. We often are drawn to meditating in front of the ocean, or looking at the sky because it contains the color blue. Blue brings calmness.

We can easily associate color with emotions, with frequencies, with Mother Nature, and as you pay more attention to the way of nature, you can begin training yourself to associate the color of fruit and vegetables and your environment with your personal needs. If, for example, you have a day when you're down and depressed, try meditating in front of the ocean, or go for a long walk and look at the sky. You can bring your balance back by opening the points of energy that feel heavy or stuck and bringing stability into your frequencies. We suggest you eat all the color frequencies during a day.

Wearing Color

There are seven major colors: red, orange, yellow, green, blue, indigo, and violet. There are seven major frequencies corresponding to these colors that you can observe in the world around you. When we dress colorfully, we are drawing on our intuitive knowledge that certain colors make us feel certain ways. In the field of psychology, there is even a form of therapy that uses color, called chromo therapy. You literally heal by using colors, by paying attention to the colors that you eat or the colors that you wear.

In ancient times, we used to pay a lot of attention to color. We wore colors to empower us. Even today, people in positions of power must have an awareness of color. The Pope dresses in white because white represents supreme peace and acceptance. Queen Elizabeth often dresses in gold or yellow, which represents solar energy and royalty. Think of the Golden Age of Greece or Atlantis where they all dressed in gold. The Ancient Egyptians also wore a lot of gold. Royalty wore gold jewelry all the time, because gold is the only molecule shaped in the form of a pyramid. The pyramid represents stability. If you want to meditate and bring stability to yourself, create a pyramid by sitting in the yoga position and imagine all the chakra points of energy aligned.

Adapting the Food Pyramid to the Wheel of Nature

We also suggest you eat "pyramid" food. For a long time, experts have been advising people to create food pyramids, to put all the major food components in the form of a pyramid in order to know what to eat. Why a pyramid? Traditionally, the pyramid has been used as a symbol of stability. It has even been used as a symbol of the way the body functions. When you think about it, the body itself — sitting cross-legged, for example — has the shape of a pyramid. In Chapter Eight, Nutrition for Maintaining and Losing Weight, you will find a modern food pyramid based on the latest research. By now most people are familiar with the concept of a food pyramid, which shows you what foods to eat in what quantities.

Our food pyramid is included in a Wheel of Nature, in order to show how our intake of food needs to be adapted to our natural physiology. We are designed to move, to "hunt for food," to spend large amounts of energy on a daily basis looking for food. This physiology is millions of years old, and in evolutionary terms it has hardly changed at all. Incorporating our Food Pyramid in a Wheel of Nature integrates, in a flexible way, our need for food with our need to be constantly on the move, just like a wheel is designed for movement. Within the wheel, we have included all the types of exercise that our forefathers did naturally in the process of looking for food, when they were hunting, running, fighting, climbing, gathering, digging, etc. You get the picture! Now we're mainly watching TV, exhausted from sitting, talking, driving. At most, when we eat at home, we take a meal out of the freezer and put it in the microwave, concerned about how many minutes it will take!

How Does the Adaptation Work?

We suggest a basic distribution of food: 30% carbohydrates, 30% protein, 30 % fat. As we said above, this is a flexible model. It needs to be adapted to the general level of movement and exercise in your life, and ideally also in each particular day. The body is always in the present, and nothing in nature is static. That's why we are presenting a dynamic model which you can tailor-make to fit your particular needs. For example, on the days when you exercise more, carbohydrates can go all the way up to 50%, while protein and fat go down to approximately 25% each. Carbohydrates are your main fuel when you exercise and are active. Otherwise you'd be burning lean muscle tissue, which is the worst thing you can do for overall health and weight loss.

Healthy living means eating from nature, eating colorful meals of fruits and vegetables, and eating everything in moderation from every food group: fruit, vegetables, whole grains, seeds, nuts. Looking back to the Bible and the time of Jesus, when he mentions giving food to people, he refers to two food groups: bread, which in those days was definitely whole grain, and fish. Why bread and fish? Because these were the major components we ate at that time to stay healthy. We had no idea in those times about cholesterol levels, and other problems associated with our diets. I also don't believe that people were as depressed in those times as we are today, although I can't prove that. I believe that today, sometimes depression can be linked to the presence of foreign chemicals in our food and in our environment, not to mention all the medications that we are taking.

Spend More Time in Nature

Some of the disturbances that exist in the world today come from the fact that we don't live enough "in nature": we don't exercise in nature; we don't have time to enjoy nature, or to work with nature. How amazing it is to go to a park and hear the birds singing in the morning, to walk under the trees, to be at the ocean, or a running stream. These are major elements in nature that we need to include in our daily routine, and remember how good it feels to go back to our source of life. Mother Nature is the source of life. We must honor, love and protect Mother Nature because she is our means of survival.

Eating Fish versus Eating Meat from Mammals

When Jesus talks about eating fish, he refers to eating products that are cold-blooded and do not have a limbic brain. The limbic brain is present only in mammals and creates a direct connection with us humans on the level of the brain. That's why when we look at a dog or at a cat, we have an immediate sense of connection with them. On the other hand, when we look at a fish or a snake, we do not get the same sense of connection.

We kill a lot of animals for food and we indirectly eat things that are not karmically good for us, because when you eat an animal that you've killed, karmically, it is not so positive, according to the universal laws. But we've been practicing this for a long time, and it's not going to be easy to get rid of this practice. We've killed animals for thousands of years. Consider how the Romans or Vikings used to eat, killing and eating animals in savage ways, and how their karma, in the end, was so negative.

Remember karma is the Number One law of spirituality. This is a book about integrating spirituality as part of your health. One way you can do that is by eating more from the original source, and not eating so much dead meat. Or eat more "white" meat, such turkey and chicken, in moderation. When you eat blood from other sources, you add a different frequency to your own frequency. If you can avoid that, you can purify your blood. For instance, if you have a blood transfusion, you add a different frequency to your own frequency. We've known this about blood transfusions, but sometimes we need them to survive.

Every single individual on Earth, never mind what blood type they have, has a unique blood frequency, just as unique as our fingerprints. It is never the same for two people. So even if you receive the same blood type, it's at a different frequency, and that might even modify your personality. (This is also true for heart transplants.) I've seen people after a blood transfusion, and their personality was definitely modified. This is a philosophic way to look at our health, and to relate to some of the changes that are affecting us at this stage of evolution.

It is important, as I mentioned, to dress colorfully, to pay attention to the colors in your home, and learn to associate the health and emotional issues that surface, with colors that you eat. Again, when looking at a particular problem, you should think which color frequency you need to eat in order to shift the vibration that is harmful, such as avoiding red meat for blood pressure, or avoiding green if you have kidney problems.

Exercise

Another important way you can return to Mother Nature is to return to your body, and be aware of how it needs to move. In the world today, most of us live very sedentary lives. We are not the nomads we were thousands of years ago, when we used to walk and migrate from one place to another. Now we stay in one place: we sit, we have cars, and we don't move our bodies. We sit at work in front of the computer, we sit at home in front of the TV, and that's how we spend each day. Some of us exercise, but a lot of us don't. Living this way is so stagnant; it can lead to a shutting down of the body's normal functions. The body needs to move, to move, to move! The body is a form of energy, and energy moves and transforms.

As we mentioned earlier in the book, our bodies are mostly made up of water. When you don't move, you literally sit on your emotions and personal issues, and you actually accumulate more water. So if you don't give yourself any regular exercise or something physical to do, each day you wake up fatter. If you are active, however, and move, you "melt" the excess water by sweating it out, and eliminate it from your body.

We know for a fact that exercise alters the chemicals of your brain. Anyone who goes to the gym every day, or just walks every day — doing the 10,000 steps a day recommended by experts, for example — is guaranteed to sleep better, have a better attitude in life, be more stable in their emotions, and feel more content. When we do something physical, we establish a connection between thinking and the body. We reconnect these two parts. You can also walk as a form of meditation — the walking mediation. Walking or being at the gym allows you to focus on your body's movement. Many times we repress our bodies. Over and over again the body gets repressed, and one of the ways is by not moving. When you don't move the body, you tend to ignore it, yet you expect it to perform all of its functions anyway.

The body needs help from us to stay strong and in balance, and maintain a healthy circulation. The more you move, the better it gets; the less you move the worse it gets, and the more stagnant you will get in your emotions. Walking, for example, is a way to release feelings and emotions. The word "emotion" even has "motion" in it, because e-motions are meant to move through us, not to get stuck. Walking works as effectively as any other form of meditation, such as a sitting mediation, to contemplate. You don't necessarily have to contemplate to release your worries. You can do it while walking and accomplish two things at the same time. You burn calories, and bring back the feeling of being alive that is so good.

The Young Generation

Young people in their teenage years should be encouraged to get involved in all kinds of sports and exercise, because teenagers tend to be very emotional. When you become a teenager, that's when you discover the world of emotions. As a young child, you tend to be unaware of your emotions, but as a teenager you wake up to the fact that we are emotional beings. We come from a drop of emotion, from a drop of water, from DNA. This is who we are. When we tap into our emotions in our teenage years, we can suddenly become overwhelmed by them. We don't really understand what's happening to us, and we end up doing a lot of harmful things because our emotions dominate us. The hormones also begin to wake up in adolescent bodies and contribute to the feeling of being overwhelmed.

When a person is overwhelmed by emotion, the first thing that happens in the physical body is that you trigger an addictive pattern or an addictive personality. That's one of the reasons that you see teenagers taking drugs or engaging in destructive behavior that hurts them physically and mentally. They have no concept of what they're doing.

If you want a teenager to choose a healthier lifestyle, and avoid addictions, you must encourage them to exercise to release their feelings, so that they can pass through this phase of life in a healthy way. Once they start exercising more, or integrating sports into their lives or any regular activity that makes them get up and move, they will find it easier to express their feelings and release their emotions. Such changes will also help to reduce the number of youth today who are dealing with the emotional and physical crisis of being overweight, at this most formative time in their life (See "Tips for Teenagers").

Addictions

Every day I work with addictive personalities who engage in compulsive behavior and/or substance abuse. Often what I notice is that people become self-destructive the very moment they cannot handle their emotions. Their self-destructiveness is demonstrated in different ways.

People are always seeking comfort; they want to reach a state of joy and happiness, but sometimes when looking for a friend who will make them happy, that friend is a substance: alcohol, drugs, pills, cigarettes or food. As these substances hijack the brain's natural reward system, people can become dependent on this artificially induced joy and happiness. However, this pleasure is self-destructive. People then count on this so-called friend to produce their joy and happiness in life, and as a result, they don't have any real friends or goals. They believe, often wrongfully, that they are not supported by the world or society, by their parents or their friends and neighbors, so their belief feeds their addictive pattern.

When this destructive cycle is in play, it's very difficult to get someone to break their behavior patterns. One therapeutic tool I use for working with people in this situation is to do a "burial." We bury the cigarettes, the food, or the alcohol. We also work on seeing how that kind of "friend "is actually your enemy.

I also use hypnosis for healing addictions. I have clients who are severely overweight, weighing 280 to

400 pounds, who don't want to die, but they cannot stop eating because food is their best friend. Food is everything they have. Their lives revolve around food. When you become that overweight, everything in your life is out of balance. With severe addictions, you have to do a "flip-flop," and begin to hate what you love most: You must begin to strongly dislike your "best friend," so that you can get rid of it forever or at least put it in its place. With food, you have to make a healthy new "friend."

HOW TO IMPLEMENT GUIDING PRINCIPLE #6: RETURN TO MOTHER NATURE

"Let food be your medicine and medicine be your food."
— Hippocrates

How do I fit eating well into my busy schedule? I don't have enough time as it is!

This may be the first reaction that many people have at the thought of changing how they eat. It's true that it will take time to shop, to investigate parts of your supermarket where perhaps you haven't been before, to prepare the food, to cook it, and clean up afterwards. On the other hand, rather than thinking what it takes from your time, think what it gives to your life. Realize that it can be an opportunity for mindfulness, for connecting with one of the most essential building blocks of our life: the food we eat. It can also be an opportunity for togetherness, for shopping or cooking together, and of course, eating together.

Give eating and nourishing your body the time and attention it deserves.

*"Eating should not become just one more item
on a list of multitasks."*
— Danny Meyer, NY restaurateur

This is not just about what you eat but also about _how_ you eat. Ironically, the so-called "more developed" countries are eating less and less well. There are increasing problems of people being overweight, including children, with all the health risks attached to that. In the U.S., 65% of adults are obese or overweight. Somehow as we become more "advanced" we seem to treat our bodies less well, as if they aren't really important. Nourishing and nurturing ourselves properly is not just a health problem — it's also a happiness problem. We need to get back to basics and look after our bodies, both in how we eat and how we exercise.

Light and Life: Go Out and Play in the Sun – It's Good for You!

The discoverer of Vitamin C, Nobel Prize Winner Albert Szent-Gyorgi, states that the energy that we take into our bodies ultimately comes from the sun. In moderation, the sun is good for keeping us healthy in many ways. For example, Vitamin D can only be synthesized in the body with the help of sunlight. This vitamin is essential for calcium absorption and therefore vital to our bone health. Calcium is the most predominant mineral in our body, and here we can see a clear link between the presence of sunlight in our lives and our general health. It has been noticed that in northern climates, where for many months during the winter the rays of the sun are too short to be beneficial for humans, a widespread presence of osteoporosis existed, compared with other countries.

Even artificially created sunlight has been proven to reduce or even cure depression, the so-called SAD (Seasonal Affected Disorder) syndrome in Scandinavian countries. For example in Helsinki, Finland and in Stockholm, Sweden there are "light cafes" where you can go and have a cup of coffee while bathing in artificial sunlight. In Scandinavia you can even get a prescription from a doctor for sunlight therapy!

Many people with eczema and other skin conditions notice that their skin improves with moderate doses of sunlight. In his book *Natural Cures They Don't Want You to Know About,* Pierre Trudeau lists 50 natural cures for more than 50 specific diseases. Very many of them have sunlight as a part of the cure!

Originally, the human race developed in Africa, and our physiology was dependent on the presence of sunlight all the year round in order for us to function at our optimal level and enjoy total health.

Tips for Teenagers

There aren't many courses in home economics anymore. Many teenagers come home to an empty house and have to fix their own meals. They also may not have healthy role models at home. They spend a lot of time in malls and around vending machines. Let's have a quick look at what could be some of the smarter choices there, and at some general tips for being healthier:

— Always leave something on your plate. Portions, especially in America, tend to be way too big.
— Share your dessert with a friend – or two friends!
— Skip the French fries, or at least share one portion with a friend.
— Have a veggie-burger instead of a meat burger. You'll be surprised how good it tastes.
— Have a veggie pizza. Eat half and take the other half home.
— Go for grilled anything, rather than fried.
— If there is a whole grain option, for bread or pasta, choose that.
— Skip the soda pop and cola. Learn to like sparkling, flavored mineral water. Think of a soda as a dessert, loaded with sugar, and to be kept more for "special occasions."
— Learn to snack on healthier options: unsalted,

preferably raw, nuts and seeds; dried fruit; fresh fruit. Always carry some with you in your bag.

— Always include protein with your carbohydrates. Understand that all carbohydrates turn into sugar (glucose or other sugars) in your body. This raises your blood sugar. Slow that process down with protein, for instance, soy burgers, fish, tofu, beans, lentils, chickpeas, chicken, and turkey.

Vitamins, Minerals and Supplements

Generally, we should be able to get our needs met by nature. However, given the lifestyles many of us lead, we don't always eat well. Also, the Earth is in many ways less nutrient rich, and therefore the foods we eat may not contain all the nutrients we need. In general, we recommend a good multivitamin as "insurance."

Think of What You *Won't* Have to Suffer Through!

Again, rather than trying to motivate yourself with fear of negative consequences, focus instead on what you get to skip, what you won't have to suffer through, when you eat real food: You will avoid weight gain, ill-health, sugar-rushes, bad experiences at the dentist, clothes that feel uncomfortable, vitamin deficiencies, high blood pressure, high cholesterol, etc.

Eat Real Food

"Real" food is natural food that comes from the Earth. In the U.S., and in Western "developed" countries, people have a lot more choices available to them — but many actually _choose_ junk, and less healthy foods. So much of the modern manufactured and processed foods that are on the shelves in your supermarket are in fact "fake foods." These are foods that will give you mostly empty calories and leave you deprived of essential nutrients.

It is actually now a selling point to label a product with "Made from natural ingredients" or "All natural!" How is it possible that we have made "food" from anything _other_ than natural ingredients? Those kinds of products really should have another name so that it is easier for consumers to know what "real food" is from a natural source, and what is processed and refined, masquerading under the label "food."

It's ironic that when people spend thousands of dollars to go to a health farm to get healthy or lose weight, they will be paying a lot of money to go back to eating healthier, more simply and naturally — vegetables, whole grains, pulses, fruit, fish (and small amounts of meat or dairy products) — just like the people living in less-developed countries! They will also be eating refined and processed foods as little as possible.

Living Food

Always include something raw at each meal. At lunch and dinner include a salad, at least as a side dish. When cooking, choose the method of cooking that destroys the least nutrients, which is: steaming, boiling lightly, stir-frying, or sautéing. Cooking in the oven may be delicious, and cooking in the microwave may be convenient, but these methods leave fewer nutrients in the food, so always be sure to have a fresh, raw salad as well.

The Golden Rule: The more processed or refined food is, the less often you should be eating it. Any kind of cooking/heating is processing.

Be in Nature — See the Animals!

If you live in the city, go to a park, have plants/flowers in your home, take home a shell from the beach or stone from your walk. We use medium-sized stones collected from various holidays as paper weights, just to add something beautiful. Have art or a pretty poster of a nature scene on your wall. When the real thing is not possible, such as in a hospital room, even a picture of nature has been shown to have a beneficial effect on patients. If the patient can be near a real window and see nature from there, even better! Children also need to be in nature. Many children living in cities have never even seen a grassy field.

"A thing of beauty is a joy forever."

— **Keats**

Weight Loss

This is not a diet book or a book primarily about weight loss. However, Mother Nature did not intend us to be obese, nor did she intend for us to be sedentary. Our bodies are designed for movement. As we mentioned earlier, over 65% of the population of the U.S., as well as many people in other countries in the "developed" world, have a problem with weight.

If you want to lose weight, or maintain your weight, here are some suggestions:

1. Eat your last meal of the day early. For example, stop eating by 7 p.m. If you get really hungry after that, have fresh fruit. In old Romanian wisdom, there was a saying, which literally translates as: "Eating at night makes you fat!"
2. Choose whole foods, meaning whole grain breads, pasta, rice, etc.
3. Increase the amount of protein in your diet.

4. Eat three meals and two to three healthy snacks daily.
5. Eat so you feel full and satisfied, but do not overeat.
6. Put cutlery down between mouthfuls.
7. Chew your food well.
8. Do not eat while watching TV. Eat mindfully and pay attention to what, and how much, you are actually putting into your body.

Stress Hormones and Your Weight

Most of us have more or less stressful lives. However, running on adrenaline means running on the wrong fuel: Adrenaline is designed to help us in emergencies and in times of crisis. It was never meant to be an everyday fuel, and used as such; it will ultimately break down the body.

Other stress hormones, such as cortisol, have now been shown scientifically to lock fat in place. While stressing, the body gets the message that there's a crisis and switches itself onto a fat-storing program. This is the body's way of ensuring long-term survival. The body doesn't understand your crisis is just a deadline you have to meet.

Eating Colorful Foods

In British nutritionist Dr. Gillian McKeith's blockbuster

TV show "You Are What You Eat," she shows "before" and "after" pictures. Before their eating makeover, people were mostly eating beige, white and brown foods, mostly processed and "dead" foods, with little or no fresh vegetables and fruit. Dr. McKeith gathers what they've eaten for a week and shows them. The sight of it all together is a shock for most people. Then she shows them their food future: A table that is laden with colorful fruits, vegetables, and whole grains. It looks beautiful and we see how people's instinctual reaction is one of positive attraction. This shows that we are programmed to eat that kind of food. The colors themselves are meant to attract our attention and signal that they are good for us to eat.

Whole Foods

"The more processed the food, the less frequently you should have it."
— Lisa Young, Ph.D., nutritionist and author of *The Portion Teller: Smartsize Your Way to Permanent Weight Loss* (*O Magazine*, August 2005)

1. Eat whole foods and foods with a low GI (Glycemic Index), the "good" carbs. Avoid the white stuff. The kinds of foods to look for are whole grain breads, pastas and rice, and other options such as quinoa, buckwheat, and oatmeal.

2. Start cooking more of your own food at home. This way, you will learn more about what you are putting into your body.
3. Get your nutrients from real foods. Avoid modern "fake foods."
4. Go for organic options as often as possible. Look for the organic section in your local supermarket. If you can, go to a store like Whole Foods Market (see wholefoodsmarket.com for a store near you).
5. Take a good multivitamin as "insurance."

Tips for Digestion

Why do we need antacids? Why do so many people suffer from constipation, complain of heartburn and indigestion? Did God make a mistake and give us bodies lacking something vital? Or are we abusing our systems and not allowing our digestive systems to do their work?

Here are a few tips to help with your digestion:
1. Food combining: Many people find that food combining helps. This idea was popularized by the book *Fit For Life*, by Harvey and Marilyn Diamond many years ago. An example of something that we have found works well is to eat your protein only with vegetables. Try having a piece of grilled fish with salad and

steamed vegetables. Skip the potatoes or the rice.

2. Eat fruit on an empty stomach

3. Chew your food well so that you begin the digestion process with the saliva in your mouth. Ideally, your food should be more or less "liquid" by the time it passes to your stomach and to the second stage of digestion. Chewing your food will also have a beneficial side effect in helping ward off gingivitis and other gum diseases. Maybe that's why "an apple a day keeps the doctor away."

4. Exercise

5. Turn off TV and telephones, and eat food in a calm environment.

Everyday Exercise

Learn to see the opportunities for exercise in your daily life. Here are 10 Tips on how to include more:

1. Get a pedometer. The general recommendation is to reach 10,000 steps per day. The average American takes only 2,000 – 4,000 steps in a day! The pedometer is a little like a personal trainer. It gives you feedback on how you are doing, inspiring you to do more. A pedometer is inexpensive and very simple to use. Also, no special equipment or clothing is required, although good shoes, e.g., trainers, are recommended. If you are not used to exercise, build up gradually. For

example, start by adding a hundred steps a day. If you are very overweight or unfit, start with just walking to the end of the block, then around the block, etc.

2. As you become more fit, you may want to add more "strenuous" steps, such as going up flights of stairs, increasing the speed at which you walk, or swinging your arms. Later, you can even add wrist and ankle weights. Getting fit may take some time: Be patient and respectful with your body. "10,000 steps a day keeps the doctor away!"

2. Take the stairs instead of the elevator.

3. Park your car further away at the mall and walk.

4. Get off the bus or train one stop earlier and walk.

5. Leave the golf cart, get a "caddy" on wheels, and walk the course!

6. Put on your favorite upbeat song and dance around your apartment — alone or with your family.

7. If you need to contact someone in your company, go see them instead of sending an email.

8. Look at chores, especially cleaning the house, as an opportunity for a work out. (You will be surprised how many calories are burned doing the dusting and vacuuming.) Put on some great music to make this more fun.

9. If you want to meet with a friend, suggest that

you take a walk together, rather than sit in a cafe. If you take your walk in the park, you get the additional bonus of fresh air and contact with nature.

10. "Shopping is my cardio!" One of the characters in the popular TV show, "Sex and the City", said this and we all laughed. But actually, it's true! You'll be surprised how many steps you take just doing your grocery shopping, not to mention shopping for clothes, shoes or anything else.

Earn Screen Time

Many people, adults and children, spend a lot of time in front of different screens: TV screens, movie screens, computer screens, video game screens, and the screen on their cell phone. Most parents find it hard to get their kids to watch less TV. Instead of nagging them, another approach is to agree that the kids have to "earn" screen time by doing something physically active, preferably outside. So perhaps, a half hour or an hour of physical activity, a walk, playing ball, going for a cycle ride, or cleaning their room, "earns" an evening hanging out with friends and playing computer games. The same idea can work for adults as well, of course. If you're going to watch a movie on TV, make sure you go for a walk first.

The Paradox of Health

We've cured many of the big killer diseases in the Western world, such as TB, cholera, smallpox, and polio, yet there are more doctors and dollars spent on health care than ever. Human suffering hasn't decreased. Western medicine can achieve — and has achieved — marvels, especially in the area of surgery and emergency care. However, the focus of internal medicine is often to "zap the bad guy" with pharmaceuticals. Unfortunately, there are often serious side effects to prescription drugs. For example, the drug thalidomide, which pregnant women took for depression, ended up having the serious side effect of deforming the fetus. Another example is estrogen, which has been widely prescribed for menopausal women. Now a serious link with breast cancer has been found and there is a lawsuit pending against the drug companies who pushed these "wonder drugs."

Lifestyle changes incorporating healthy eating, exercise and stress-reduction have proven to go a long way in lessening the effects of, or even eliminating, an impressive number of modern medical conditions. These include: osteoporosis, high blood pressure, high cholesterol, insulin resistance, diabetes, depression, menopausal symptoms and even some forms of cancer.

Chapter Seven:

Guiding Principle #7: Create Good Karma Every Day
Embrace Responsibility

This book, as we said before, is all about creating a healthy lifestyle, improving your thinking, improving your habits, making your life ideal, and translating your life into a dream life. And it is absolutely possible! We have covered the principles of awareness, being proactive, finding balance, finding joy in life and togetherness, and returning to Mother Nature. Now we will explore how everything in our life relates to our karma and our ability to embrace responsibility.

We come from a drop of memory, from our DNA. Our DNA creates every component in us: the way we look, the color of our skin, how tall we're supposed to be, what we do with our skills and our abilities. It's everything that's within us. Now as we grow in the physical world and form our bodies and our emotions, we are tuning into the memory of our cells. Our cells contain karmic memory — things of the past.

Karma is a very old concept. I talked about the idea of karma in my first book, called *Everyday Karma.* In that book, I refer to karma being the number-one spiritual law, the number-one law of the universe, the law of cause and effect, the law of your actions, the law of your thinking, and the law of your memory. *Everything that you implement on a daily basis comes back to you for resolution.* Whatever you do to others comes back to you so that you can grow and better understand yourself, your thinking and your actions. Whatever you do to your own self stays within yourself to be resolved.

As I've said before, many times in life we take wrong actions towards ourselves, we repress ourselves, we treat ourselves badly, pretending that it doesn't matter. Everything matters! Everything adds up to everything! And everything is in a process of transformation. If we look in the mirror, we never look the same from one year to another. We change and we transform. The body transforms as its molecules transform and regenerate. I learned from Deepak Chopra, for example, that the liver regenerates every 30 minutes, producing new cells. Our whole system regenerates! So we need to take this into consideration, along with all the principles of karma, and the fact that the memory that you create by your actions is significant because it stays within you. We need to be healthy. Therefore, we have to take healthy actions. We have to think healthy thoughts. We have to create positive karma towards everyone. But you cannot create positive karma for those around you if you aren't creating good karma for yourself.

What does "good karma for yourself" mean? It means treating yourself right. Loving yourself is part of creating good karma: appreciating yourself, never letting yourself down, building your self-esteem, working on your beliefs, and working on giving birth to you. I mention several times in my first two books that we are here on Earth to tune into ourselves. This is the first goal of being alive: to go through the school of life and learn about ourselves. And if you learn about yourself, definitely, the first thing you'll do is to begin to shift any negative karma that you bring from somewhere else, and any negative vibration that is within you, and turn these into something positive. It is possible to change our individual karma, and then indirectly change your family karma and the global karma as well. What the world needs today is to shift the collective consciousness, and indirectly shift the old karma of the Earth that has existed for the last 2,000 years. This is the era of Kaly Yuga, a very bloody era on Earth, during which we created a lot of destructive things. These are still reflected in us, and they still come up in us for resolution and change. So everything that humanity is facing today is still our old karma coming up for healing.

How are we going to change global karma by changing ourselves individually? We need to start by treating ourselves with respect, by believing in ourselves, doing our work and learning our lessons. It's also very important that we take responsibility for every action. This is responsibility towards yourself, and indirectly, responsibility to the world. You have to be responsible for your family. You have to be responsible for the future. You have to be responsible for the next generation on Earth. When you think this way, then you begin to see the bigger picture on Earth. Seeing the bigger picture will open your mind to a larger perspective, and open your thinking to a bigger vision. We all should have a vision!

We are all a particle in the infinite universe. Therefore, as I mentioned before, we should live within universal laws. If we live within universal laws — for example: the law of love, the law of wisdom, the law of integrity, the law of dharma — then we not only create very positive vibrations, but also very positive memories. And that's how you create positive karma. "What comes around goes around"

— this has been translated into the Newtonian law of Cause and Effect.

So "what goes around comes around" — that's the principle of life. Life is a circle, life moves, life transforms; life is "samsara", the mandala, the circle of survival. And any time you're within the circle, you tend to go to the center of the circle in order to be able to free yourself from everything within the circle and resolve your issues. And how are you going to resolve your issues, if you don't acknowledge them and take responsibility, if you're not working on the things that are out of balance in your life? How are you going to live a healthy life if you're not paying attention to your wrongdoings, if you're irresponsible, if you challenge the perfection of the universe? How are you going to be a happy person, if you go to the gym or eat the right food but your actions and thoughts are negative? If you're obsessed with negative thinking, then you're not able to apply the law of unconditional love, and are incapable of resolving your issues with your family. Then you're not a participant in the big picture of the world, which we all should be.

We must all wake up to the realization that we have to come forward to serve the world in whatever way we can. Whether we work for the post office, or are teachers or presidents of countries, we're all here to serve the beauty of the world and to bring peace. That's what the world needs. Peace, Healing, Wisdom. When that happens, life on Earth will become healthy and positive more easily. We're not going to destroy Mother Nature any more. We're going to treat the people around us with more love and compassion. We're going to treat ourselves better. What you do to yourself you should do to others.

Unfortunately, many of us don't treat ourselves right, and that is reflected in our relationships. If you're not good to yourself, if you don't treat yourself right, it's easy to understand that you're not going to be capable of treating others with total compassion and forgiveness. Forgiveness and compassion — these are still lessons to learn for humanity at this point. They are still part of that big picture of health. And as I've mentioned, it's so important for your own well-being to detach and forgive yourself and others. Detach from bad vibes, from bad feelings you have towards the people around you, no matter what they did to you.

After 2,000 years, we should have learned from the teachings of Buddha and Jesus who taught us not to hurt anyone, regardless of what they did to you. This we need to say over and over again as part of the healthy principle of survival, of prolonging our lives. It's not enough just to take care of your body. You must also take care of your thinking and your spiritual evolution on Earth, because every single day of your life, you create more karma. Every single day of your life, by design, you're meant to go on to another lesson. Waking up in the morning means waking up to another lesson and learning something different, and trying to apply something different. If you're reluctant to learn, those lessons will haunt you and return again and again for the rest of your life!

Our general tendency is to blame the world around us, and not acknowledge that the problem exists within ourselves. Creating good vibrations begins early in the morning by the way you eat, by the way you think, by the way you program your day. So start the day by making a list of all the positive things you want to accomplish during the day. Try to put something good in the world; try to do something good, gentle and positive for any living creature around you. For example, do something good for an animal or for a beggar at the corner of the street. That's going to make you feel good. This is going to give you what's called a "helper's high." When you show yourself that you are capable of doing good to others, you'll feel good.

In my opinion, life must be planned in order for you to create a positive life. You need to set goals for positive behavior, involve yourself in organizations that serve the world to whatever extent you can. You're not going to feel depressed if you're active for the good and lead a dynamic life. Life is all about being active and dynamic. It's not about stagnation. Stagnation actually means killing the source of energy. Life is all about energy that moves. Life is about thinking — because what we think, we become. The world around you is a manifestation of your thinking.

Reality reflects what the mind projects. So make sure that you have a very positive attitude towards your physical body, and also have a positive attitude towards your thinking. Acknowledge your thoughts. In the world today the media is responsible for relaying information to large groups of people. There are TV channels about food, exercise, buying and selling. By comparison, there are very few programs that talk about spirituality, that teach people how to empower themselves. There are few ways in which the media teaches people how to tune into themselves, how to open up to their skills and abilities, and therefore, be open to possibilities.

As I've said before, when you evolve from that drop of DNA, which is your memory, it works like data in a computer. Everything you are is already in place there. If you work on those parts of you that were formed in the beginning of your life, then you are working on your sacred contract for being here on Earth. You have to work on what you agreed to be here for. Even before being born, we made an agreement. We came with a mission. From day one, we've known exactly who we are, on some level, even though we didn't know how to talk yet! There is so much about ourselves that we must work on and investigate, in order to create the life that's meant for us. And we all want to have a happy and healthy, positive and powerful life.

Karma and Your Body

Now, the last subject I want to address in this chapter is the relationship between your karma and your body. The memory of your physical body lies in the memory of the cells.

When I was five years old, I nearly drowned; I almost died in the hospital because I couldn't breathe. Interestingly enough, later on in life when I learned about hypnosis and I got my Ph.D. in Hypnotherapy, that incident came back to me. I had a fabulous doctor teaching me, and during a session, he asked me what happened when I was five years old. That question transported me into another life, where at the age of five, I had died in a large house surrounded by a lot of toys. That memory came back in my present life at the age of five.

Everything you've experienced at a specific time in your previous lives, at 12, 20 or 70 years of age, will come back to you as a memory of something you've experienced before. It will be revealed again to you in some new experience. The body will tend to go through the experience of the previous life. This is how the memory gets activated in that particular moment. And something that you've been through can come back to you over and over. Karma means going through different lives and different incarnations in a physical body. That's why it's important to create good memories so that in your next incarnation, if you choose to come back to Earth, you can live healthy and happy. Then your mind will be free from trauma and bad experiences of the past.

That's why hypnotherapy is such an effective tool for healing. There are many ways to heal not only the body but also the mind. Hypnotherapy is definitely one tool that can help you erase phobias and negative memories of the past that are located primarily in the right hemisphere of the brain. It is because of this that I say that it *can* happen that you live a perfect life, that you have perfect health, and do everything right. You can become that person who the whole community loves, and have a good relationship with yourself, your family and the people around you. In other words, you've reached the stage of almost doing things perfectly in this imperfect world. But at some point in life you might get a disease, a karmic disease. And that karmic disease comes from somewhere else, from another incarnation.

I once met a woman who used to work for a big TV network, as a producer of a popular show. She was in her 50's when she came to me, wanting to do a TV show based on psychic and paranormal phenomenon. She wanted to do a session with me first. I'll never forget looking at her and saying, "There is a spot on your left lung." She said, "I don't know what you're talking about." I asked her if she used to smoke in the past, and she said "Yes, but that was a long time ago." I told her "Still, you have to check your lungs." In my vision, that woman had had lung cancer in a previous life. Interestingly enough, three months later she was diagnosed with lung cancer, and she unfortunately died soon after that.

We have to make sure that we activate memories of the past to prevent tragic occurrences that are part of past lives to not hit us again as hard as they did in prior experiences. So always take care of your memories, of what you remember, so that your memory cells don't tap into your physical body and cause a sudden illness, tragedy or misfortune. Your karma and your body is a big link between your memory and the current events that are happening to you. Karma is calcified within your cells. It stays within you. Sometimes it's even transferred to other generations. Karma definitely means the memory of everything you've ever experienced. If in another life you've been a teacher or composer, that also might come back to you at some point in your life. I find it interesting that I started writing my first book at the age of 40, and I believe that being a writer probably came from a previous life. The way I started singing on stage at the age of seven also came from another life.

Everything that taps into the physical body — all your skills and your abilities — relate to karmic issues that will be revealed at some stage in life. Pay attention to who you are. Investigate more, do regression work on any obsessive patterns, or any phobias that you might have, or if you have any recurring dreams. Tune into yourself and tune into your future. My whole philosophy is that the future is something that you can have some control over. And that's positive. *If you want to have a healthy future, you should always know what's happening to you in the present, and what's happened in the past.*

HOW TO IMPLEMENT GUIDING PRINCIPLE #7: CREATE GOOD KARMA EVERY DAY

"Everywhere people ask, "What can I actually do?" The answer is as simple as it is disconcerting — we can, each of us, work to put our own inner house in order."
— E. F. Schumacher, *Small is Beautiful*

Make Conscious Choices

How are you living in the world, what choices are you making? We are the result of the choices we make. For example, choosing to skip meals, choosing to eat junk food, choosing to drink excess alcohol, all of these have consequences. Understand that when you choose a certain course of action, you also choose the consequences.

Buddhism shows us how to create more compassion and suggests choices that lessen the suffering in the world. Buddhist teachings say, "Don't kill to eat," so some examples would include compassionate farming, and eating more plant-based foods. Buddhism suggests not drinking alcohol because of the suffering that excess alcohol causes in the world; physical, mental and emotional suffering. Another reason is environmental: The revered Buddhist monk Thich Naht Hahn points to gigantic quantities of rice that would feed large populations in Asia being used to make rice-based alcohol instead.

Organic Foods – Good For You, The Farmers, And The Environment

By choosing organic food whenever possible, you are contributing to your own health, and also the health of the farm workers. Many farmers in the western world, who choose to turn their farms organic, do so because they want to avoid contact with chemicals. For example, bananas not treated with chemicals are better for the farmers and workers, as well as for you, the consumer.

Embrace Your Responsibility

1. To Yourself
2. To Your Family
3. To the Coming Generations
4. To the World

Your Responsibility to Yourself

— Take the time it takes to eat well and exercise, and to relax.

— Find the time to become aware of how you choose to live your life on an everyday basis. Start designing your life in a conscious way rather than being reacting to everything that happens to you. For example, start a journal and begin to record your thoughts and feelings.

— Plan goals for positive behavior.

— Visualize your goals.

— Be more active and dynamic; plan what you intend to achieve on a daily basis.

— Perform random acts of kindness.

— Meditate

Your responsibility to your family

— What lifestyle habits are your children learning from you?

— What are you and your kids eating? "Honey, We're Killing the Kids" is a line from recent American television, from parents who realized the catastrophic long-term consequences of the food they were putting on the table.

Your responsibility to future generations

— The 7th generation argument: If we don't look after the Earth NOW, the 7th generation will not inherit a fertile beautiful Earth. The Native Americans believe that when making a decision or making a choice, we should first consider how it would affect future generations.

Your responsibility to the world

— Support Fair Trade organizations. The Fair

Trade movement is devoted to paying workers in developing countries a fair price for their produce. Look for the "Fair Trade" signs on foodstuffs such as chocolate, coffee and other imported goods.

— How we treat other living creatures. There are also questions of our responsibility toward other living creatures, such as the animals we eat. Religious people sometimes say, "Well, it says in the Bible that we can eat meat." But we wonder if God meant us to "factory farm" his creatures, to feed them on the dead and diseased bodies of other animals, to transport them for long distances in ways that, at the very least, are uncomfortable? Although most people are caring human beings, there doesn't seem to be time in the busy day to necessarily eat in a way that would help our planet.

— Don't underestimate the power of small changes Even small changes, when they reach critical mass, that is, when they are being implemented by a large number of people, will create significant positive changes. For example, only a few years ago it was hard to find whole grain options in your local supermarket. You had to go to a special health food shop. Now, not only are these whole grain options available pretty much everywhere, but they are also often organic and reasonably priced.

— Use your power as a consumer. Just don't buy junk food! Additionally, become a sugar detective. If you start looking at the content of "hidden" sugar in a variety of everyday products such as bread and breakfast cereals, you will be shocked. Alarmingly high amounts of sugar are available even in so-called "healthy" products such as protein drinks, energy bars, and meal-replacement drinks. Stop buying these products and preferably let the manufacturers know why. If manufacturers can't sell their products, they will be forced to adapt them to meet consumers' needs.

PART TWO:

HOW TO EAT HEALTHILY — AND JOYFULLY!

Introduction to Part Two

Part Two introduces our food pyramid and gives you the necessary tools to apply it to your everyday life. It gives you our main tips that will help you restructure your environment and your schedule in order to accommodate healthy lifestyle changes.

Based on state-of-the art research, and also on the way certain cultures eat that have proven to be healthy, we have collected a number of eye-openers in order to create understanding of what works best for our physiology and what leads to health and joy for your whole life.

Why include more meat-free and dairy-free foods in what you choose to eat?

You will see that our food pyramid is grounded in largely vegetarian/vegan food. The reason that this book will focus mostly on plant-based, non-dairy food is that most people don't really know where to begin with making that change in their diet. They don't really know what's available, and how delicious it can be, as well as how good it is for them and the environment. We know there are lots of books with recipes for meat eaters. There are also quite a lot of vegetarian lifestyle books. This is the first book that bridges the gap by suggesting mostly plant-based options aimed at meat eaters who would like to include more "green" in their diet, but who don't necessarily want to "become" vegetarian. I consider this to be a very _inclusive_ book.

Including more meat-free and dairy-free eating in your life is beneficial to both the human body and to our environment. It's a way to "tread lightly on the Earth." Livestock and livestock grazing are a major factor in the depletion of water resources. Rain forests have been cut down to provide land for grazing or for raising crops such as soy beans, which are then transported, sometimes long distances, to be fed to livestock in other parts of the world.

Part Two is for YOU if you've ever had any of the following thoughts:

"I really would like to include a bit more plant-based food in my diet, but I don't know how. It seems so complicated — hours of boiling beans!"

"I really should reduce my cholesterol."

"What on Earth am I going to cook for a vegetarian who doesn't eat dairy? Help!"

"My friend is lactose-intolerant. What can I give him to eat?"

This section is for everyone, whether you eat meat often, rarely, or already are vegetarian. The purpose is to introduce you to easy, delicious plant-based meals — that also happen to be nutritious and healthy.

We've talked to a lot of meat eaters, and they say the main reason they would eat more plant-based food is for health reasons. The benefits of including more non-dairy, plant-based foods are many. For example:
— Lower blood pressure
— Lower cholesterol
— Healthy weight loss
— Better digestion
— Prevention of cardiovascular disease
— Prevention of diabetes
— Prevention of stroke

However, within a mainly plant-based, non-dairy nutritional lifestyle, we also recommend fish (especially fresh fish), moderate amounts of "fresh," white, less-processed cheeses, for example, feta cheese, goat cheese, mozzarella. Also, there is room for moderate amounts of eggs (especially egg-white omelets), chicken (skinless, grilled) and turkey.

We have found that being flexible and inclusive makes life easier and more joyful!

Nutrition for Losing and Maintaining Weight

MAIN CONCEPTS

The Body is Always in the Present

Physiologically, your body is always in the present moment. It will benefit from every healthy choice you make and it will suffer from every negative choice you make. Being in the present moment, the body doesn't understand your mental strategies, such as skipping a meal to save calories for a later meal. The only thing the body understands is whether or not it's getting enough food for survival in the present moment. Therefore, the moment you skip a meal, or don't eat enough, the body switches itself onto a lower metabolic rate, burning less calories, in order to conserve energy. It also switches onto a fat-storing program to ensure your survival long-term. The human body has been running on this programming for hundreds of thousands of years. It has not adapted to our modern way of living, where food is available in large quantities most of the time.

So when you've skipped a meal in order to save calories and then "pig out" in the evening, the consequences for the body are exactly the opposite of what you had hoped for: You will store most of the food as fat and will end up gaining weight. The Sumo Wrestler diet was designed along the same lines; the young wrestlers eat little during the day and then have a large meal before they go to bed.

Crucial Need for Structure

If you want to lose weight and maintain the weight loss, creating a structure in your life is crucial. This structure will be different for different individuals; however, some sort of organization is key to your healthy whole life. What kind of structure are we talking about? For example, the structure of _when_ you are going to eat. Many people have a disorganized and stressed life, and just grab anything. Make sure you get up early enough in the morning to have breakfast and to exercise in whatever small way you can. If you have other tasks to do in the morning, such as getting the kids off to school, training yourself to become an early-riser is essential. Plan your food shopping so you always have healthy food options in the house. Recent brain research even shows that the people who learn to become more organized have greater success in losing and maintaining weight.

Go Slow to Go Far

Be patient! If you want to lose weight, allow at least 8 weeks before you expect to see results. Weigh and measure yourself at the beginning of the period, and then again after the eight weeks. NOT BEFORE! Focus on long term loss, rather than a quick fix. Your focus is to be a healthy weight your whole life, rather than going on a fad diet and putting on all the weight again after a few months. In fact, if you are very overweight, it may take one to two years to finally get to your target weight. Allow nature to take its time. Trust your body and the process of creating a healthy lifestyle. The seed does not become the flower overnight. There is a natural process of development and change that takes a certain period of time. How long it will take in each case of losing weight is highly individual.

In fact, you don't even want to lose weight at all! You want to lose fat! If you just focus on losing "weight," what you are losing might be muscle mass, bone density or just water. What you want to lose is excess fat.

OUR FOOD PYRAMID
Adapting the Food Pyramid to the Wheel of Nature
BASIC MODEL
The basic model we recommend is
30% carbohydrates
30% protein
30% fat
What we mean here is _energy percent_ that is the amount of calories that come from the food you eat. Don't mix this up with _volume percent_, which refers to the quantities of the food that you eat. For example, in terms of volume percent, vegetables may occupy 50% of your plate, but

yield only 5-10% of the calories. On the other hand, a small amount of salad dressing occupying 5% of your total plate volume may yield as much as 30% of the total calories in your meal!

Adapting the Basic Model to your Individual Needs

Our food pyramid is a flexible one, allowing for differences in the distribution of energy. You need to assess, on a daily basis, how to make this flexibility work for you. On days with more physical activity, you will need to raise the carbohydrate percent. For example, if you train hard at the gym, and go for a walk on the same day, you may need to increase your carbohydrate percent all the way to 55%. On the other hand, if you don't move so much, cut down on your carbohydrates and raise your protein percent instead. Actually, the flexibility is mainly between the carbohydrate and the protein percent. We recommend that the fat intake — of good, healthy fats — stays stable around 25-30%

Carbs	Protein	Fat
50%		
↑		
30%	30%	30%
	↓	↓
	25%	2

THE FOOD PYRAMID

FAT

Animal	Vegetable
Fatty	Oils, e.g.,
fish, e.g.	olive oil,
salmon,	flaxseed,
mackerel, eel	rapeseed
	Nuts, e.g.,
	walnuts, almonds
	Seeds, e.g.,
	pumpkin, sunflower,
	sesame

PROTEIN

Animal	Vegetable
Fish, e.g., fatty fish, tuna,	Tofu
snapper, grouper, bass,	Other soy products: burgers,
etc.	sausages, breakfast patties,
Chicken (skinless, grilled)	soy milk, roasted unsalted
Turkey	soy beans
Eggs (mostly egg-whites)	Quorn (a mushroom-based
	protein product)
	Lentils and beans
	Other bean-based products,
	e.g., hummus, falafel
	Protein drinks (sugar-free!!)

COMPLEX CARBOHYDRATES

Fruit & vegetables	Whole grains (low GI)
Take your pick!!	Whole grain pasta
Don't forget things like berries and dried fruit	Quinoa
Eat a rainbow everyday!	Brown rice
	Small amounts of couscous, bulgur, polenta

A Comment on the Food Pyramid: Vegetarian/Vegan

As you will notice, apart from fish, and small amounts of chicken, turkey, fresh cheese and eggs, we recommend eating lots of vegetarian and even vegan foods. This is supported by some of the latest research that suggests that to be a "fish-eating vegan" is the most beneficial way to eat, and is in line with our physiology. For example, Swedish celebrity nutritionist and author Fredrik Paulun highly recommends this way of eating.

It is also in line with how some of the older cultures in the world traditionally eat, for example, Japan. Also, Mediterranean countries such as Greece eat lots of fruit, vegetables and fish, while eating minimal amounts of dairy and moderate amounts of meat.

The Wheel of Nature is Your Daily Exercise

The exercise you can get every day falls under four main categories. Make sure you get a variety of exercise within a week.

1. Fat-burning

Walking is by far the easiest and the very best. Ideally, do it in the morning, before your day begins.

2. Strength training / muscle maintenance and development

In order to protect your muscle mass, and burn even more calories, we recommend 2-3 weight-training workout sessions a week, at home or at a gym.

3. Cardio

This basically means increasing your heart rate above your normal level and starting to sweat. This can include power walking, jogging, biking, swimming, Stairmaster, aerobics, dance, etc.

4. Everyday exercise

This is the most underestimated form of exercise! Everything from opening doors and carrying groceries, to taking the stairs and cleaning the house, burns significantly more calories than you would think, and helps to make you fitter. Become an everyday exercise detective. Seek out the opportunities — and take them! For instance, park your car a little further away at the mall or supermarket, and walk. Get a pedometer/step-counter. You will be surprised how many steps accumulate during the day.

Get a Support Group behind You

Remember Principle #5, Treasure Togetherness. Exercise will be much easier — and more fun — if you have a support group behind you, even if it's just one buddy. If you can get your family involved, that's wonderful. Another form of everyday exercise is playing with your kids!

OTHER PRACTICAL TIPS AND USEFUL IDEAS

Food is Not Your Enemy — "Fake" Food Is!

Learn to understand the difference between "real" food and "fake" food. Become a detective with a mission: to identify and rule out fake food from your life and the life of your family. Find it and chuck it out from your fridge, from your cupboards, from your trolley at the supermarket, from your menu choices at the restaurant. Even from the dinners you go to! Like Dr. Phil says, "Program your environment for success." If that ice cream you love so much is not in your freezer when you're hungry, you won't be able to eat it!

Make Sure you Eat Enough Protein

Fish

Tofu

Other soy products: burgers, sausages, breakfast patties, soy milk, roasted unsalted soy beans

Eggs

Quorn (at health food stores and some supermarkets)

Lentils (found in Indian restaurants)

Beans (found in Mexican, and South American restaurants)

Other bean-based products, e.g., hummus, falafel

Chicken and turkey

Protein drinks (read the label!! Stay away from sugary products.)

Stay Ahead of the Hunger

Learn to stabilize your blood sugar and stay ahead of the hunger. The moment your blood sugar drops, the body will send you powerful signals to eat immediately in order to raise your blood sugar. In that biological condition you will not be able to make healthy choices.

Educate yourself about the Glycemic Index

The Glycemic Index (GI) is a tool that will help you understand what foods to eat in order to keep your blood sugar stable. This index was originally developed to help diabetics understand how the food they eat affects their blood sugar levels and therefore their overall health.

Certain foods you eat, for example processed, refined carbohydrates (e.g., white bread) will cause a sharp increase in your blood sugar in a short time. High blood sugar levels are dangerous to the body. In order to bring them down to a normal level, the body then produces high amounts of insulin. Insulin is a fat-storing hormone which, long-term, leads to excess weight and obesity. This is an extremely simplified explanation of the Glycemic Index.

However, what you need to do now is familiarize yourself with a good Glycemic Index table (for example, the one in the South Beach Diet). By doing that, you will be able to choose foods that keep you on the healthy side of the Glycemic Index, and you will learn to keep your blood sugar stable. Stable blood sugar is your best friend when it comes to losing or maintaining weight. It is a great indicator of overall health.

Stay Away from Sugar

Choose natural sweeteners like honey & maple syrup.

Stock up on dried fruit: apricots, prunes, dates, figs.

Have bowls full of fresh fruit such as berries, cherries, strawberries, grapes, etc.

Re-connect with Nuts and Seeds

Establish a healthier Omega 3/Omega 6 balance in your body. One way of doing this is to consume small amounts (a small handful) of nuts and seeds daily. This can include:

Walnuts (richest in Omega 3)

Brazil Nuts

Almonds

Pecans

Hazelnuts

Pumpkin Seeds (richest in Omega 3)

Sunflower Seeds

Sesame Seeds

A note on the Omega 3/Omega 6 balance:

When we emerged as a species, the ratio of the essential fatty acids Omega 3/Omega 6 in our food was 1-to-1. Nowadays, in the diet of most Westerners, it's 1-to-20! This imbalance is considered, by many scientists, to be one of the main sources of inflammation in the human body.

Eat Enough Fish

Eat fish 2-3 times a week. Go for fresh, especially from the oceans. Don't be afraid to include "fatty" fish, such as salmon, mackerel, eel, etc., on a regular basis. Along with nuts and seeds, the fatty acids from fish will re-establish a healthier Omega 3/Omega 6 balance in your body. This ratio is of great importance when maintaining your overall health. For example, it will help you reduce and prevent inflammation of the body.

There is now enough scientific evidence to support the fact that the fat that comes from nuts and fatty fishes, when eaten in moderation, does not make you fatter. On the contrary, it seems to help you burn your own fat deposits more effectively.

Eat Breakfast

We recommend some form of gentle exercise before breakfast in order to take advantage of the fat burning mode that body is still in after a night of not eating. However, at most, you should wait an hour before eating breakfast.

Eating breakfast is extremely important, and in many ways, it is true that it is the most important meal of the day. Breakfast will also increase your metabolic rate. This, in conjunction with exercise, will give you a high metabolic rate at the beginning of your day which sets the pace for the rest of your day. It is like giving your body instructions for how to perform during the remainder of the day. Why is a high metabolic rate good? because it burns more calories all the time, even when you rest or sleep.

The composition of your breakfast is important. Give yourself enough protein and include foods with a low Glycemic Index. This also sets the tone for how your body will perform for the remainder of the day and gives you a platform for a stable blood sugar throughout the day.

Having a late breakfast or skipping breakfast altogether is one of the worst things you can do. Remember, the body is always in the present moment and doesn't know that you are planning to eat a big lunch. It will put you in starvation mode, lower your metabolism and store fat for you instead.

The 80/20 Rule

The 80/20 rule says that you can eat anything and everything — as long as 80% of the time you stick to healthy guidelines. The remaining 20% of the time, you can pretty much do what you want! In practical terms, this can translate into six days of healthy eating and one day a week when you have the freedom to choose exactly what you want. This one day a week will not affect you negatively. On the contrary, you will avoid psychological deprivation and be more successful long-term. Or you can do the 80/20 ratio on a daily basis if that works better for you.

Within your 20%, when you decide, for example, to have dessert, go for high quality and great taste. Have a homemade wonderful dessert made of natural ingredients. Go to a fabulous bakery that has a good reputation and where you know they make desserts from scratch. Eating is supposed to be a joy, so food should also taste delicious. On the days when you choose to drink wine, treat yourself to a high quality wine and savor every drop.

Be Inclusive

Our whole philosophy in this book is to be inclusive, rather than excluding things and denying yourself. Rather than thinking you have to exclude something to eat healthily, think inclusively: How could you include healthier meals in your family's diet at least once a day?

Rather than thinking "What can I throw away?" think "What can I add that's healthy and delicious?" Add more fresh and dried fruit, add more nuts, because then automatically the less healthy options will diminish in quantity and in frequency. They'll simply have less space in your life.

Take the Best and Leave the Rest

There is something in the paper almost everyday about different ways of eating: Glycemic Index, South Beach Diet, Atkins, good carbs/bad carbs, food combining, Paleolithic diet (i.e., what our Stone Age ancestors ate), and so on. There are also diets for your blood type. All of these have a value and are interesting to look at. Our approach is to be eclectic: to take the best and leave the rest. What can we learn from each of these different methods that make sense in a healthy lifestyle not just for a few weeks or months, but also for your whole life?

Don't be Cheap! Invest in your Health!

How much is it going to cost to include healthier foods in what you choose to eat? We'll be honest: Often, the organic alternative is going to be a little more expensive. However, consider the long-term savings in terms of medical insurance and preventing human suffering. Our vision is that, rather than the healthier alternatives being hard to find, they will, in fact, soon take up most of the store while the junk food will be in the "minority" section. How long will this take? That's really up to all of us. We can start by making more choices that value ourselves, and the amazing organism we are.

In practical terms, what could you do each day? Maybe you start by substituting organic bananas for regular, out of solidarity for the workers. You skip the chemicals — and so do they!

We encourage you to think about the quality of all the food you eat. When choosing eggs, meat and fish, choose the best quality, because it's both good for you, and good for the planet.

"The Leaping Salmon" – Allie's aunt and uncle in England live near a river with a pub on its banks called "The Leaping Salmon." This is how fish — or any other animal – are supposed to be: living in their natural habitat, able to move and enjoy their lives, not pumped full of hormones, or trapped in a fish farm where they can only swim back and forth!

When it comes to fish, choose fresh fish (not frozen), and fish caught in the wild, such as wild North Atlantic salmon.

When choosing fish, meat, eggs, cheese, milk, think about the following:

How has this animal lived?

In the case of farm animals, has this animal felt the sun on its back?

What has the animal been given to eat?

How far and by what means has it been transported?

How was it slaughtered?

Food Combining

From food combining, we've taken the idea of eating fruit on an empty stomach. Also, when drinking coffee, we generally take it on an empty stomach. (See resources for book suggestions on these ideas.)

However, as a general rule of thumb, we have found the following formula helpful. Make sure that at each meal you have:

A grain-	-a pulse**-	-and a vegetable
Rice (Whole Grain)	Lentils	Broccoli
Pasta (Whole Grain)	Beans	Carrots
Couscous	Peas	Lettuce
Bulgur	Soya Products	Leeks
Potatoes	Tofu	Peppers
Polenta	Quorn	Cabbage
Bread (Whole Grain)		French Beans
Buckwheat		

**NOTE: Instead of the "pulse," you could have an animal source of protein, such as fish, turkey or chicken*

Wonderfoods

Include one or more of the following "wonder" foods each day in what you eat:

1. Quinoa
2. Soy products (tofu, soy milk, etc.)
3. Olive oil (cold-pressed, virgin)
4. Linseed oil
5. Broccoli
6. Avocado
7. Fresh, wild-caught fish
8. Nuts and seeds
9. Lentils and beans
10. Berries

Summary of Eating Tips for your Whole Life

— Eat lots of fresh fruit and vegetables, preferably organic, and/or locally grown.

— Eat whole grains.

— Eat pulses (beans, lentils, chickpeas, etc.).

— Eat soy products (tofu, soy milk, soy mince, and soy casserole chunks).

— Eat fresh fish.

— When you wish to eat meat, be moderate and choose the highest quality, organic, leanest meat, mostly white meat, such as turkey.

— When you wish to eat dairy, be moderate and choose the highest quality organic, fresh, artisanal cheeses, e.g., feta, goat cheese, mozzarella.

— Think of cheese and red-meat more like dessert! Eat it sparingly, one or two times a week, and in small amounts.

— Limit the amount of processed or refined foods in your diet.

— Eat so that you are full and satisfied, but not "stuffed." Do not overeat.

— Eat three good meals (breakfast, lunch and dinner) and two to three healthy snacks a day.

— Have dinner early (the earlier the better).

— Savor your food: Eat fairly slowly and chew well.

— Cut down on coffee and fizzy drinks.

— Cut down on alcohol. Just one drink a day is good for you. After that, alcohol is counter-productive. Think of that one glass of wine also as dessert, something to be savored and enjoyed.

— Drink plenty of water.

— Choose high quality sweeteners, such as honey, brown sugar. If you're going to go for dessert, go for something really delicious, rather than snacking on lots of small things.

Chapter Nine:

How to Choose Delicious and Nutritious Meals Every Day

WHAT TO HAVE AT HOME

Here is a list of foods for the fridge and store cupboard, so that it's easy to have the necessary ingredients for healthy cooking. For example:

OILS:

At home, we have four oils in the fridge:
— Cold-pressed virgin olive oil (for dressings)
— Cold-pressed canola/rapeseed oil (for cooking)
— Linseed oil (as an Omega 3 food supplement)
— Sesame oil (after cooking, to add flavor to for, example, Asian dishes)

Use virgin olive oil for salads or for when you really want the taste of olive oil. We use organic rapeseed oil when we're frying something. With salads, we like to try a variety of oils, such as a mixture of virgin olive oil, linseed oil and cold-pressed canola/rapeseed oil. We recommend taking one spoonful of linseed oil in the morning as an

Omega 3 supplement. (If this is difficult, you can take the oil in capsule form instead.)

"Pure," "cold pressed," "virgin," "extra virgin" — what does it all mean? "Pure" sounds good, but read the label carefully. The oil may be heat-treated and more processed. All that "pure" means in that case is that it is not a mix of two kinds of oils. Look for these descriptions on the oils you buy: "cold-pressed," "virgin," "extra virgin," or "expeller-pressed." Your local supermarket brand may be just as good as the more expensive brands. Just check the label carefully.

SAUCES

Sweet and sour sauce — Look for brands that are low in sodium and with no MSG (monosodium glutamate), and no artificial preservatives.

Soy sauce — this is high in sodium, but adds great flavor to cooking. Look for the lower sodium varieties.

HERBS AND SPICES

There are all sorts of herbs and spices you can use. Here are some of our favorites:

— Whole seed cumin
— Ground cumin
— Basil
— Thyme
— Paprika
— Cayenne
— Ground ginger
— Cinnamon

RICE AND OTHER GRAINS

— Whole grain rice

— Whole grain pasta

— Quinoa pasta

— Plus Pasta: Enriched multigrain pasta

— Couscous

— Buckwheat

— Polenta

— Quinoa

— Amaranth

— Whole wheat flour

— Bulgur

TIP: Make at least double the quantity of rice (couscous, polenta, etc.) that you need. Use the leftover rice to accompany your meal the next day.

A word of warning! Except for pasta and quinoa, everything on this list has a relatively high Glycemic Index. Therefore, eat moderate portions, preferably in combination with protein. This means in practice, don't just eat a mountain of pasta. Have a smaller portion of pasta, with, for example, veggie meatballs.

BEANS & CHICK PEAS

Have a variety of beans and lentils at home, both in tins and also in packets to prepare from scratch. If you have tins, carefully check that they contain as little sodium as possible, and no sugar. If possible, buy organic.

For example:

— Kidney beans
— Small white beans
— Giant white beans
— Black-eyed peas
— Black beans
— Adzuki beans
— Mung beans
— Red lentils
— Green lentils
— Yellow lentils
— Channa dal

Beans from scratch:

There are lots of beans available in cans, and this is by far the easiest — yet still fairly nutritious — way to use them, as long as the sodium content is low. However, if you do make beans yourself, you will find that they taste better. Here are a few tips:

1. Make a whole packet of beans each time. What you don't use, freeze in smaller portions in freezer bags. Why smaller portions? We have found that "a little goes a long way" when it comes to beans!! Also, you can add some beans to a vegetable casserole, stew or soup to make a highly nutritious and delicious meal.

2. How do you know when beans are done? Generally, the cooking times given on the packet are rather optimistic. Perhaps the manufacturers don't want you to be put off! (If you are put off, just buy a can!)

3. One of the main complaints about beans is that they are "indigestible." The following tongue test will help you know if the beans are ready: Press a bean up against the roof of your mouth with your tongue. If it "yields," it is ready. If not, cook longer.

READY-MADE MEALS

It's always better to cook from scratch. However, most of us don't have lifestyles which make that possible all the time. So stock up on the healthiest ready-made meals available, preferably frozen. Check the label. Look for organic, high quality, low fat, low sodium, and low sugar versions of items such as:

— Vegetarian chili
— Spicy Black Beans
— Veggie Lasagna
— Veggie Chicken
— Veggie Veal Schnitzel
— Tofu Steaks
— Veggie Meatballs

NUTS & SEEDS

Look for raw, unsalted, organic nuts, such as:

— Almonds
— Hazelnuts
— Brazil Nuts
— Cashews
— Pecans
— Walnuts
— Sunflower Seeds

— Pumpkin Seeds

— Sesame Seeds

DRIED FRUIT

Look for the organic, natural varieties that contain no added sulfur. In apricots, for example, this will mean they have a darker brown-orange color, rather than the light, bright orange. For example:

— Raisins

— Dates

— Apricots

— Figs

— Prunes

— Dried Apple Slices

AT THE SUPERMARKET

Spend some time getting to know your local stores and supermarkets. The following suggestions come from supermarkets we've explored in New York and Florida. We have also included suggestions from health food stores. However, in order to make it as easy as possible to eat more healthily, the products really need to be readily available, and that probably means your local supermarket.

In this supermarket section, we have mentioned some products by name. We want to point out that there are many great companies offering great products, so explore your local supermarket for what is available in your area.

Our reason for mentioning specific products is to make it as easy as possible for you to get started.

"To boldly go where no man has gone before."

Exploring your supermarket may take time, perhaps even hours! So you might want to take it one aisle at a time. It will also take time to check out labels and find out what is actually in the products you are looking at. The upside is that when you have done this once, and found products you like, you can easily and quickly find them in the future.

Each supermarket is different. In some we found whole grain pasta and other natural foods in the "Ethnic" section. In others, they are near the fruits and vegetables. Or, just look in the "boxed pasta" aisle. Go to the dairy section for cheese and milk alternatives. Once you've found them, it'll be easy the next time.

"If you always do what you've always done, you'll always get what you've always got. Dare to change!"
—(Source unknown)

FROZEN MEALS

As much as we recommend cooking from scratch, (because you know exactly what you're eating), we also know that that's just not realistic all the time, or even most of the time. Fortunately many manufacturers are producing great ready-made vegetarian options. If you look for the plant-based options, these will all be cholesterol-free.

MEAT SUBSTITUTES

"Fresh" food such as veggie grounds or tofu, are often found in a refrigerated section near the fruit and vegetable section. Frozen versions are usually found near the frozen vegetable section of the supermarket. Meatless breakfast options, such as veggie breakfast patties or veggie dogs, may be found near the other frozen breakfast foods. Go on a treasure hunt in your store!

— Veggie Chick'n Tenders (for using in your own recipes)
— Veggie Chick'n Nuggets
— Meatless Pepperoni Slices (for pizza toppings)
— Meatless Meatballs
— Veggie Steak
— Veggie Burgers (South Beach Diet-recommended)
— Smart Bacon "Pig Out Intelligently!" as it says on the Lite-Life product
— Veggie Hot Dogs (Morningstar, Boca)
— Deli Slices In Ham, Turkey Flavors
— Chicken Substitute (Boca Chick'n)
— Tofu: available in many different varieties: Silken Tofu, Extra Firm For Grilling, Stir Fry And Sautéing
— Tofu Grills
— Ranch Flavor Veggie Dip

DAIRY SUBSTITUTES

Usually found either near the fruit and vegetable section, or in the regular "dairy" section.

— Soy Cheese Slices (Veggie Slices: good source of calcium, cholesterol and trans-fat free)

— Grated Soy Cheese (Veggie Shreds)

— Veggie Parmesan

— Soya "Kaas" Cheese (comes in different flavors such as soy mozzarella) is lactose-free, cholesterol-free and a delicious natural cheese alternative.

— Butter Alternative (veggie butter alternative — cholesterol and trans-fat free, as well as a source of Omega 3)

— Vegetable Spreads: e.g., Fleischmann's, made with corn oil. Try the unsalted version if you need to cut down on sodium,

— Another great alternative is just a spoonful of virgin olive oil on bread or toast.

— Soymilk (Organic Silk soymilk: "Calcium-enriched and vitamin-fortified, free of lactose, cholesterol, gluten — and worries! You still have to pay for it though," as it says on the container of 8th Continent Soy Milk. Low fat and an excellent source of calcium. Makes a great dessert and is recommended by the American Heart Association. Helps lower cholesterol and may reduce the risk of heart disease.)

— Soy creamer

— Almond and other nut-based milks

WHOLE GRAIN OPTIONS – THE "GOOD" CARBS

"Diets rich in whole grain foods and other plant foods and low in total fat, saturated fat and cholesterol may reduce the risk of heart disease and certain cancers."

—(Source unknown)

152 *Ronzoni Healthy Harvest Whole Wheat Pasta*

Recommended by the American Heart Association. Excellent source of fiber, no sodium, cholesterol-free. Whole wheat pasta is available as thin spaghetti, wide noodle style, and linguine.

Bulgur Wheat

Versatile whole grain food, high in dietary fiber, 0 cholesterol. No additives, no artificial ingredients. As they say on the box, "Food made the way nature intended." Low in fat, rich in "B" vitamins and minerals. More nutritious than rice and pasta. Try the Heartland brand.

Couscous

We suggest Hodgson Mill whole wheat couscous with milled flax seed and soy. All natural, low fat, high fiber; 450 mg Omega 3 oils per serving

Quinoa

Quinoa is a South American grain, loaded with protein. It was used by the Incas 5000 years ago. Quinoa is being heralded as "the Super grain of the future." Try the quinoa grain itself, which cooks like rice, or quinoa pasta by Ancient Harvest.

TIP: Most of your shopping should be in the outside aisles of the supermarket, where you will find most of the fresh foods!

TIPS FOR EATING OUT

* Skip the bread at the beginning. Be proactive and ask the waiter not to bring it! Bread, especially white bread, is very high on the GI scale. You're really better off having a small dessert instead!
* Ask for dressings and sauces on the side.
* Ask for the small bottles of olive oil and vinegar so you can make your own dressing. Often, this will be lower in calories and better for your health.
* Go for grilled, steamed, stir-fried, broiled, seared, or baked foods.
* Have a good source of protein, e.g., fish, skinless, turkey breast, tofu, or beans.
* Ask for brown rice.
* Ask for whole grain pasta.
* Beware of portion sizes! Often one portion is enough for two. Share, or eat half and have the rest to go. Or ask for a half portion.
* Share desserts 3 or 4 ways.
* Always leave something on your plate, contrary to what most of us were told growing up! Leaving something on your plate sends a powerful message to your brain that you are full and that you are in control.
* Less is more. Limit your wine to just one glass.

Chapter Ten:

Where Do We Go From Here?

HOW TO USE THIS BOOK

Change can sometimes feel overwhelming. Even helpful information that we have sought out or asked for, and know we need, can leave us asking the question, "Where do I begin?"

Here are some suggestions that will help you start your process with some simple steps.

A Principle A Day...

Looking at each of the seven guiding principles, make a plan to focus on one principle each day the week. Monday is "Awareness day," Tuesday is "Be Proactive" day, and so on.

The "One Thing" Rule

Each day, ask yourself:

What is one change I can integrate for myself/my family today that will start to make a difference?

Suggestions:

— Clean out all the junk food from the fridge so that it's easier to resist.

— Get up five minutes earlier and do breathing meditation.

— Explore the supermarket for healthy options.

— Replace white pasta with whole-wheat pasta.

— Cook a vegetarian/vegan meal for family or friends.

— Read another book on healthy nutrition.

— Pick up a health magazine.

— Share with a friend some of your new knowledge.

— Explore the web, e.g., go to www.wholefoodsmarket.com

A SEVEN-DAY PROGRAM
TO GET YOU STARTED

IMPORTANT!
CONSULT YOUR DOCTOR OR HEALTH CARE
PRACTITIONER BEFORE CHANGING YOUR DIET AND
EXERCISE ROUTINE. WE RECOMMEND THAT YOU HAVE
A MEDICAL CHECK-UP BEFORE YOU START MAKING
ANY CHANGES.

BEFORE YOU START:

These are the elements to include in your week to help you establish a healthy routine and structure for your whole life.

Create a Realistic Strategy for your Day
In order to be able follow this program, it is essential to prioritize it and make time for it in your busy schedule. A simple way to "create" more time is to get up earlier. Maybe it's worth cutting down on the amount of TV you watch late at night in order to be able to put your healthy lifestyle first. Remember that the next day starts the night before.

Lose Weight in Eight!
For healthy weight loss we recommend that you stay with the seven-day program for at least eight weeks before checking on your progress. Why eight weeks? Partly because it will take that long to see real progress, and

partly because, in eight weeks, your brain will have had enough time to establish the new habits. Remember of course that in order to get down to your ultimate goal, it could take one or two years. But doing it at a slow pace that you can incorporate into your whole life is only in your favor. Research shows that people who lose weight gradually over a longer period of time tend to keep their new weight more successfully than people who go through spectacularly rapid weight loss.

Choose an Inspiring Goal

Choose an inspiring goal that you would like to attain by the end of the eight-week program. It is best to choose something concrete and measurable. For example, you may want to get into a favorite outfit that has been hanging in your closet for some time. Be realistic here: A size 10 or 14 is more achievable than a size 4! Or you may want to just be able to play with your kids without feeling exhausted. Or to play golf again, or to go dancing.

Measuring Your Progress: You Don't Want to Lose Weight!! You Want to Lose Fat!

Weighing yourself on traditional scales has often led to a focus on the number of pounds people weigh. This has led to a misleading focus on quantity of pounds lost rather than quality of your overall health. It is more important for your health and for your long-term success that you learn new ways of measuring your weight.

Therefore, we recommend measuring yourself on the new type of scale that will show the distribution of fat and muscle in your body. The most reliable method is called a "BodPod." Check your local gym, fitness or weight loss center to see if they have one.

Muscle weighs more than fat, and what you need to do is to lose fat, not muscle. Your muscle mass is your best friend. Women especially need to change their culturally programmed thinking when it comes to muscle mass. All human beings are designed to have muscle in order to be strong and function well in the world. Strong is beautiful! Muscles are alive and use energy/calories all the time, even when you're sleeping. Therefore, muscle mass raises your Basic Metabolic Rate and you will be burning more calories all the time. Your fat deposits, on the other hand, are "dead" tissue, just sitting there. Fat is something that you just lug around, like carrying heavy suitcases. Excess fat is a burden on the body and it doesn't do you any good.

Your muscle mass, however, makes you lean, strong and powerful; it gives you better posture, better confidence, protects your bones, and makes you look more toned. Your muscle mass is beneficial to your overall health and well-being in the world.

It is better to be healthy and build muscle mass even if you are still a little overweight, than to be skinny. Being skinny is not insurance that the distribution of muscle and fat is a healthy one. Often, the opposite happens. For example, fashion models have been known to have a large percentage of fat on their bodies and very little muscle mass.

What is a Healthy Ratio of Fat to Muscle Mass?
Approximately, what you want to aim for is:
For men, maximum 20% fat (of your total body weight).
For women, maximum 30% fat (of your total body weight).
Note: Even if your total body weight doesn't change, by following our program, your ratio of fat to muscle will change, and then you will be on your way to better health, more strength and proper weight loss and maintenance for your whole life. Therefore, we advise you to put away, hide or even get rid of any traditional scales. Instead of motivating you, they can have the opposite effect — demoralizing you, when in fact you're making progress.

Plan your Exercise Program for the Whole Week
Remember, you will benefit most from a variety of exercise:
— Fat-burning: 3-4 times a week, preferably first thing in the morning, like walking, swimming, biking
— Strength training: 2-3 times a week at the gym, or at home: dumbbells/free weights, resistance bands, fitness ball
— Cardio/aerobic: (exercise that increases your heart rate/pulse and makes you sweat) 2-3 times a week power walking, jogging, Stair-master/treadmill, dancing, power swimming

— Everyday exercise: Take the stairs, open doors, carry shopping bags, clean the house, park further away and walk, etc.

Morning Exercise, Before Breakfast:

If you plan to have a more strenuous morning exercise session, you also need to have a protein drink. This will give you fuel and strength in order to be able to perform your exercise. Have a banana with you to eat immediately afterwards.

Generally, we do not recommend a strenuous work out first thing in the morning. We believe walking tends to work well for most people and is a gentle way to wake the body up in the morning. Another gentle alternative is swimming. Walk or swim for at least 20-30 minutes. Continue for a maximum of 40-45 minutes. Learn to stretch afterwards. Stretching maintains flexibility and prevents injuries, so do not skip it. Of course, stretching also burns calories!

IMPORTANT: If you haven't exercised for a long time or are very overweight, start with, for example, just five minutes and gradually work your way up. Listen to and respect your body!

Why is First Thing in the Morning the Best Time for Fat-Burning?

While you are asleep, the body is in "fat-burning" mode in order to keep your vital bodily functions going. This includes liver functioning, breathing, heart beating, etc. When you wake up, before you eat anything, your body is still in "fat-burning" mode. So while you walk or gently exercise before breakfast, you will be burning even more fat. The moment you start eating, the body switches to "burning food" mode and will burn the food you eat, instead of your stored fat.

It is important to understand that this only works for a short time in the morning, for a maximum of an hour. After that, if you're still not eating, the body will switch on "starvation" mode which decreases the metabolic rate and stores even more fat. See "Eat breakfast" in Chapter 8.

Start your Day with Water
Start your day by drinking a large glass of water. This rehydrates the body after the night's sleep and helps flush out toxins. Never skip this.

Then, for fat burning, drink a small cup of coffee or tea. The caffeine raises your metabolic rate and helps you burn more fat.

THE SEVEN-DAY PROGRAM

Multiply by eight weeks to "Lose Weight in Eight"

Day 1: MONDAY

Start your day with a glass, or two, of water

Morning exercise — walk — before breakfast

Breakfast

Snack

Lunch

Snack

Dinner (cut off your eating by 7 PM)

Fresh Fruit

Day 2: TUESDAY

Start your day with a glass, or two, of water

Morning exercise — walk — before breakfast

Breakfast

Snack

Lunch
You need to have a large and nutritious enough lunch in order to build up reserves for your upcoming strength-training session.

Power Snack
Again, in view of your upcoming strength training session, you need your snack to nourish you. Include a good balance of protein and carbohydrates. Have your power snack about an hour before your training session. However, keep it light enough so that you can in fact exercise. It's hard to exercise on a full stomach. Besides, the digestion process interferes with the work your muscles need to do.

Exercise: Strength-training (gym, dumbbells, resistance bands)

Dinner (cut off your eating by 8 PM)
Carbohydrates: After strength training, make sure your

% of carbohydrates is higher. It can go up to 50% (see our Food Pyramid). This is because you need to restore your depleted carbohydrate reserves. This will not affect your weight loss.

Fresh Fruit

Day 3: WEDNESDAY

Start your day with a glass, or two, of water

Morning exercise — cardio before breakfast. Have one or two bananas with you for immediately after your session, or during the session.

Breakfast

Snack

Lunch

Snack

Dinner (cut off your eating by 7 PM)

Fresh Fruit

Day 4: THURSDAY

Start your day with a glass, or two, of water

Morning exercise — walk — before breakfast

Breakfast

Snack

Lunch
You need to have a large and nutritious enough lunch in order to build up reserves for your upcoming strength-training session.

Power Snack
Again, in view of your upcoming strength training session, you need your snack to nourish you. Include a good balance of protein and carbohydrates. Have your power snack about an hour before your training session. However keep it light enough so that you can in fact exercise. It's hard to exercise on a full stomach. Besides, the digestion process interferes with the work your muscles need to do.

Exercise: Strength-training (gym, dumbbells, resistance bands)

Dinner (cut off your eating by 8 PM)
Carbohydrates: After strength training, make sure your

% of carbohydrates is higher. It can go up to 50% (see our Food Pyramid). This is because you need to restore your depleted carbohydrate reserves. This will not affect your weight loss.

Fresh Fruit

Day 5: FRIDAY

Start your day with a glass, or two, of water

Make sure you have a protein drink

Morning exercise — cardio before breakfast. Have one or two bananas with you for immediately after your session, or during the session.

Breakfast

Snack

Lunch

Snack

Dinner (cut off your eating by 7 PM)

Fresh Fruit

Day 6: SATURDAY

Start your day with a glass, or two, of water

Morning exercise — walk — before breakfast

Breakfast

Snack

Lunch
You need to have a large and nutritious enough lunch in order to build up reserves for your upcoming strength-training session.

Power Snack
Again, in view of your upcoming strength training session, you need your snack to nourish you. Include a good balance of protein and carbohydrates. Have your power snack about an hour before your training session. However keep it light enough so that you can in fact exercise. It's hard to exercise on a full stomach. Besides, the digestion process interferes with the work your muscles need to do.

Exercise: Strength-training (gym, dumbbells, resistance bands)

Dinner (cut off your eating by 8 PM)
Carbohydrates: After strength training, make sure your

% of carbohydrates is higher. It can go up to 50% (see our Food Pyramid). This is because you need to restore your depleted carbohydrate reserves. This will not affect your weight loss.

Fresh Fruit

Day 7: SUNDAY

Day of rest and recreation.

Even God rested on the seventh day. So should you! With a clear conscience.

This is your 20%.

Do whatever you want!

Eat whatever you want!

Enjoy your life!

Celebrate you successes!

Go out with friends and family!

MEAL SUGGESTIONS FOR THE SEVEN-DAY PROGRAM

BREAKFAST

Here are some suggestions for a healthy breakfast:

* Egg-white omelet with veggies
* Oatmeal with cinnamon, soymilk, nuts and dried fruit; or fresh fruit like berries
* Muesli with rice milk or any other non-dairy milk you prefer (check the sugar content)
* Granola with soymilk or any other non-dairy milk you prefer (check the sugar content)
* Pancakes made with soy and buckwheat flour; serve with slices of soy cheese or feta cheese
* Meatless breakfast patties, burgers or sausages (which have no cholesterol, are a good source of protein, are South Beach Diet-recommended, and are low fat); serve with grilled or sautéed mushrooms
* Spreads

Here are some spreads and toppings to serve with whole grain toast and vegetables, such as tomatoes or cucumbers:

Tofutti "Better Than Cream Cheese" spread (which contains no dairy, no cholesterol, no lactose, and no butterfat)

Hummus (chickpea) spread/dip

Veggie meat-substitute slices (turkey flavor, for example)

Veggie cheese

SNACKS & POWER SNACKS

Here are some suggestions for snacks:

— A handful of nuts
— A handful of seeds
— A moderate portion of dried fruit
— Fresh fruit
— A few squares of real, at least 70% pure dark chocolate

Here are some suggestions for power snacks:

— Baked beans on whole grain toast
— Good quality cereal or protein bars, low in fat, sugar and sodium
— Smoothie or soy milk shake with protein powder and berries (fresh or frozen)
— Feta cheese salad with a slice of whole grain bread
— Hummus on whole grain bread
— Small portion of whole grain pasta, with mozzarella or a few nuts
— Veggie burger

LUNCH & DINNER

Always have both raw fresh vegetables, such as a salad, and cooked vegetables, such as steamed vegetables, with each meal. In terms of volume, vegetables should fill approximately half your plate. Have a dressing of cold-pressed olive oil and freshly squeezed lemon or lime juice on your vegetables. The oil will help with absorption of the fat-soluble vitamins: A, D, E and K.

Plan to have a small portion of complex, whole grain carbohydrates with most meals: whole-wheat pasta, brown rice, etc.

Have a good look at the food pyramid. You can compose, create, and combine your meals pretty much as you wish, following the guidelines in the pyramid.

Here are some suggestions for lunch and dinner:
— Vegetarian Chili Sin Carne
— Tofu meals: Available in Chinese, Japanese, Thai restaurants. Ask for brown rice!
— Lentil and Chickpea curries: Available in Indian restaurants, when eating out.
— Pasta dishes combined with protein, e.g., meatballs, fish, beans, veggie meat sauce
— Grilled, steamed, baked, seared or broiled fish with vegetables and salad. Can include salmon, mackerel, eel, tuna, snapper, grouper, bass.
— Grilled chicken or turkey with salad and vegetables
— Tuna salad
— Veggie burger with salad and whole grain bread
— Veggie egg white omelet (IF you haven't had eggs for breakfast)
— Falafel with salad and whole grain pita bread

CONCLUSION

We hope that this book has inspired you. We hope that it has given you both the spiritual and practical guidance you need in order to be able to change your whole life in a positive direction. The changes that you make will affect everybody around you and even the world at large.

With more awareness, more joy, and more togetherness, we hope that you will be able to find more balance, and return to the basic principles of life, to the Trinity of Health, that is there to support us. In doing this, you will assume more responsibility for yourself, and for improving the world we all live in, so that we can leave it a better place for the generations to come.

BIBLIOGRAPHY

AGATSON, Dr. Arthur: The South Beach Diet

DIAMOND, Harvey & Marilyn: Fit For Life

DYER, Wayne: The Power of Intention

HARRA, Dr. Carmen: Everyday Karma

HARRA, Dr. Carmen: Decoding Your Destiny

LANZALOTTA, Stephen: The Diet Code

LOEHR & SCHWATZ: The Power of Full Engagement

MCKEITH, Dr. Gillian: You Are What You Eat

MYSS, Dr. Caroline: Why People Don't Heal And How They Can

NESTLE, Marion: What to Eat

TOHEI, Koichi: Ki in Daily Life

TRUDEAU, Kevin: Natural Cures They Don't Want You to Know About

The One-Minute Meditator: Nichol and Birchard

WILLETT, Dr. Walter: Eat, Drink and Be Healthy

ACKNOWLEDGEMENTS

Dr. Carmen Harra wants to thank her daughter Alexandra, her sister Mona and her husband Virgil, for the inspiration, as well as her parents, Alexandrina and Victor, for their divine support and love.

Carmen is grateful to Jon Sweeny and Peter Carlson for their superb friendship, and to Amazon.com for publishing this book… and to the Universe for making it a best seller.

Thank you to my editor and proofreader, Sharon Athanasiou, for her dedication, help, and enthusiasm.

Mona and Allie would like to thank nutritionists and authors Fredik Paulun and Martin Brunnberg of the Paulun Nutrition Center in Stockholm, Sweden, for all their knowledge and inspiration. Their state-of-the-art research has created a shift in our thinking and helped us write this book.

We would also like to thank our dear friend Vesna Mattsson for being a constant source of inspiration and support for the 20 years that we have known her.

ABOUT THE AUTHORS

Dr. Carmen Harra is a clinical psychologist, metaphysician, motivational speaker, and radio and television personality. She is the author of three internationally acclaimed books: *Everyday Karma, Decoding Your Destiny,* and *Signs, Symbols, and Secrets.* In addition, she is a singer and jewelry designer for QVC, and the host of three radio shows on Healthy Life, Contact Talk Radio, and Sirius Satellite 114. Carmen lives in New York and Florida with her husband and three children, and has dedicated her life to helping others achieve health and happiness.

Mona F. Muresan, Ph.D., is a Swedish certified nutrition adviser and an NLP coach. She has recently moved to America to work more closely with her sister Carmen Harra.

Allie Swain hails from Britain and is a professional lifestyle coach, certified by the International Coach Federation. She is also a certified nutrition adviser.

3638682

Made in the USA